Vectis

Also by the author

Electric Tapestry
Vectis Voices

VECTiS DAYS
Gus Jonsson

A Boy's Memories of the Isle of Wight

brandicat

Published in 2021 by brandicat
Littleborough, Gtr Manchester

ISBN 978-1-9163791-1-4

All rights reserved
Copyright © Gus Jonsson, 2021

Cover art: 'Down Shore' (detail)
Copyright © Gus Jonsson, 2009

Design by Flapjack Press
⊕ flapjackpress.co.uk

Printed by Imprint Digital
Exeter, Devon
⊕ digital.imprint.co.uk

This book is sold subject to the condition that is shall not by way of trade or otherwise be lent, re-sold, hired out or otherwise circulated in any form, binding or cover other than that in which it is published and without a similar condition including this condition being imposed on the subsequent purchaser.

*Dedicated to Ian Sherfield
and to my parents
Brenda Hazel Augustus
and Stanley Augustus*

*and with thanks for their
invaluable help and support to
Paul Neads, Dave Morgan
and my wife Rosalind.*

Contents

Author's Note	8
Foreword by Dave Morgan	9
Preface	11
In My Grandmother's House	15
Bommy Building	16
The Blue Lagoon	18
Osborne Bay Beach	23
Whitecroft Hospital	24
Time for Tea	26
Maria and Her Mother	27
Mary, Margaret and Marilyn	29
The Sketchbook	30
Beneath the Tree	35
Going Home	36
The Lady on York Avenue	39
The Table	40
Long Ago, When We Were Nippers	45
The Mystery Tour	46
Raining on the Beach	48
Knowledge	49
No Matter Sunday Morning	51
The Hercules Artisan	52
Comes the High Tide	57
The Lesson	58
Boys on Bikes	63
The King's Cinema	64
Memories of Maria	67
Cousin Ray and the American	68
Resco's	70
Down Shore	72
Up and Running	73

Christmas Day, 1957	75
Posterior Epistaxis Maximus	81
The Cannon	82
East Cowes Castle	85
The Seat of John Nash, Esq.	90
Northwood, 1954	91
Mad Masie	94
Douglas Dragonfly	99
'Never ever in your life stop reading'	104
A Field Walk to Folly	110
In a Pear Tree	111
Gypsy Girl	116
The Initiation	117
The Mire	122
The Silver Birch Tree	125
A Girl's Bike	126
The Needles	131
Peril and Plans	137
Comes the Day, Comes the Sixpence	141
Epilogue	*142*

Author's Note

To enable this volume of my story to be told, I have again chosen to utilise sketches, paintings, old sepia curling family snaps and postcards – all of which exist forever in my mind's eye. The prose and poetry of these memories of a mid-twentieth century Isle of Wight are therefore derived and documented from chronologically random remembrances.

Foreword

In *Vectis Days*, Gus Jonsson returns to the magic, mystery and misery of childhood on the Isle of Wight during the 1950s. Old favourites return but their eccentricities are matched by new faces, with particular attention paid to the friendship of a group of boys whose escapades and high-risk ventures would land them before the juvenile court or in A&E today. The casual, innocent, brutality and insensitivity of childhood is melded with an unspoken compassion and solidarity which carries the gang through a catalogue of picaresque adventures. In parallel, there is a recurrent reference to the tenderness of unaddressed infatuation, the stirrings of young love, and Jonsson's precocious ease in the presence of exciting and unorthodox young women.

Highlighting the most memorable events of a young life could portray a closed world inhabited by eccentrics and with an unending font of melodrama, without recognising the humdrum patterns of life which hold family and community together. Yet behind the cycle of seasonal ritual, the highs and lows of sweet and sour Christmases, the endless sun-kissed summer days of abandoned freedom, lie deep adult concerns of which a child is only partly aware.

The beauty of *Vectis Days* lies in its randomness and its language. Lyrical poetry and stark reportage intermingle. Mourning, madness, mirth and mayhem jostle for space on each page. Its precise attention to place may lead the reader to open an atlas (or google) to visualise the physical geography on which these vignettes are earthed. This is not an Isle of Wight of the tourist, who gets short shrift, but a view from the inside out.

Vectis Voices, the first volume of Gus Jonsson's autobiographical memoirs, left many questions unanswered and *Vectis Days* does not seek to resolve them. With no reference to schooling, as if it doesn't exist, and an early obsession with drawing dropped in casually, Jonsson is feeding us parts of the jigsaw that fit together neatly, but do not as yet reveal the full picture.

I look forward to reading more.

Dave Morgan
May 2021

Preface

Boys and bikes, sea and shingle, the tangle of leaves and branches that bid you welcome to the silence of the woodland. The pungent aroma of the wild garlic, the delicate scents of bay and pine and everywhere in the distance the sounds of the sea. Island Boys with sand in their shoes, sun-bleached tousle-tops, boys browner than berries, wearing forever summer upon their faces.

Growing up on the Isle of Wight in the 1950s, always in the company of the same small gang of fiercely loyal friends, was mainly an outdoors life; there was the sea and the river, woodland glades and abandoned castles all within a stone's throw. We made our own amusement, our own camps, we built bikes from bits. We had a unique love and zest for life, not forgetting, of course, a healthy interest in boy's toys – airguns, catapults, bows and arrows, brass shell cannons, cartridges and squibs, together with our own sand foundry for making moulded lead shot. Woe betide any other small gang of friends that wanted to knock our camp down.

We northern Island Boys only really knew West Cowes and East Cowes and the immediate hinterlands, with the two towns being separated by less than a hundred yards of river at high tide. We were territorial and tribal, but there was truly no other place on Earth more wonderful to be born into. To be known as an islander – a *Caulkhead* – has been a special privilege for which I will be forever proud.

I will eternally be part of my dear island and hold it close to my heart wherever I might be in this wonderful world. I know full well that for as far distant and long as I might travel, I will always return.

My life's progress forever improves and thus time flies, fleeting past us leaving at best snapshots, curling letters and a shoebox full of memories.

Gus Jonsson
April 2021

VECTIS DAYS

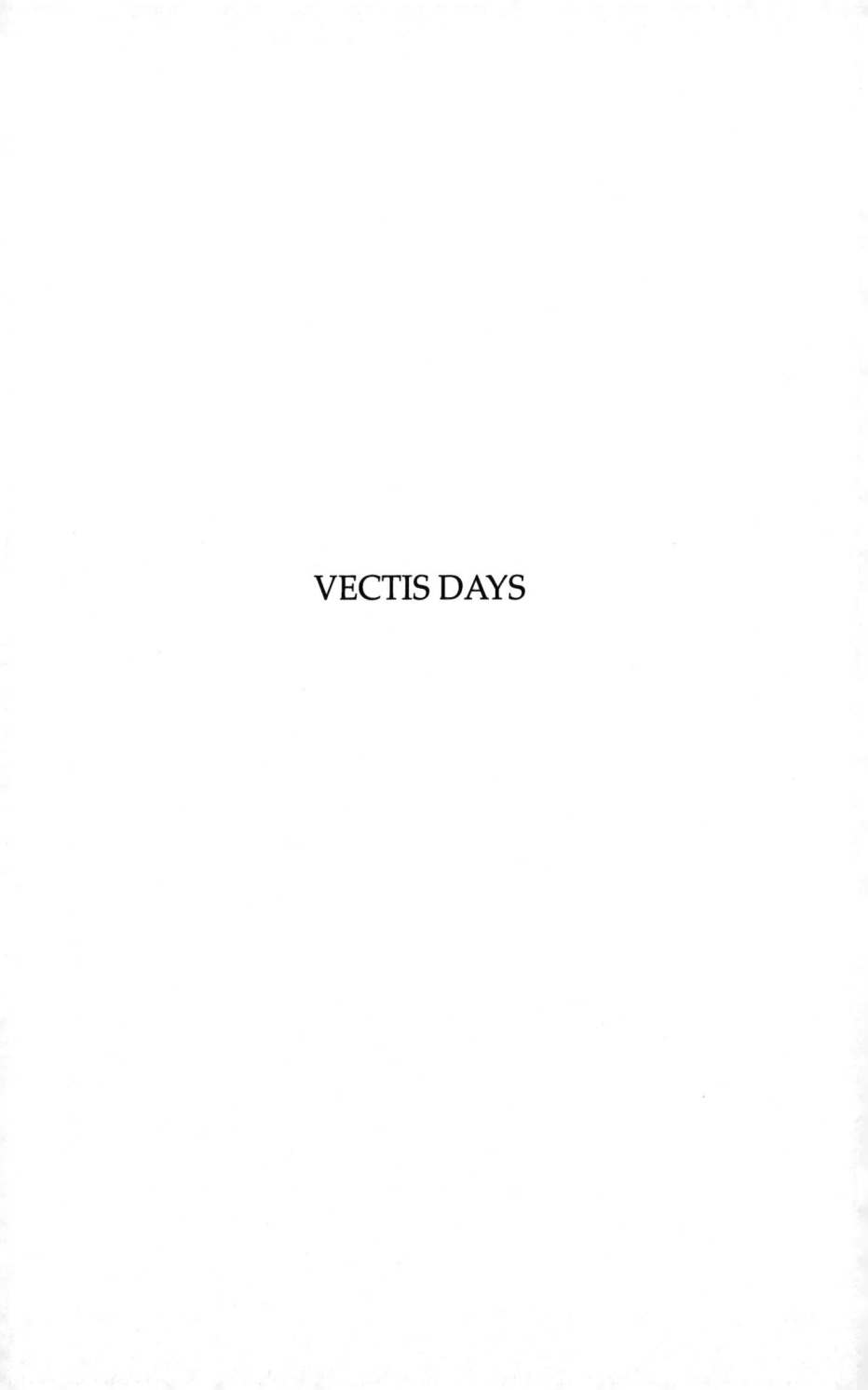

In My Grandmother's House

Just reflections in a window
Her hair
Kissing her shoulders
Jet black and shining
Like the cooking range
In my Grandmother's house
Her eyes dipping flashes of light
Her nearly-smile half-hidden
Shook the ground upon which I stood
I had to take her home with me
To stay forever
In my Grandmother's house
Maria
Just her name written on paper
Maria
I placed her name in the shoebox
Together with a thousand other memories
With a thousand postcards and kisses
In my Grandmother's house

There in the shoebox with me forever
Maria
Her name written in red
At the bottom of my bed
In the small back bedroom
In my Grandmother's house

Bommy Building

Ever since I can remember, I have always felt comfortable close to the sea. Whether in the sea, or upon its salt-kissing spray when you walk its jagged edges, or fishing or sailing. The distant shipping sounds and the pungent smell of the Solent have always been a second nature to me.

The Isle of Wight in the fifties was not as well known to me as you might expect, particularly when I was young. Northern islanders like myself knew Cowes and East Cowes. It was very infrequently that you needed to visit Ryde or Newport. Other local areas were Osborne and Whippingham, whilst down along the River Medina was Folly. They were known to us, but as for the back of the island it may as well have been abroad.

As the years went by, we older boys became a little more adventurous. We had all been able to build bikes out of pieces from the scrapyard or the abandoned bombed-out building close to the shipyards. My 'Frankenstein' was a stag horn-handled death-trap with no mudguards or lights, a fixed wheel and one very squeaky back brake. Bright yellow tape sufficed as the handlebar grips, whilst the Sturmey Archer gear cable swinging loose was wound around and tied to the crossbar. As I recall, we only had one bicycle pump between us – we quickly became very proficient at changing wheels and mending punctures. We seldom took these misfits onto the road, choosing instead to ride and jump and dirt-slide around a ruinous demolition known to us as 'Bommy Building'.

Bommy Building was, we believed, the bombed-out remains of the once grand Park House and the Olinda Villa on York Avenue, blitzed by the German Luftwaffe during the war. It was dangerous, strewn with brick and all the detritus and mangle you might come to expect from bombed-out buildings. The once ornamental gardens had overgrown into thick impenetrable jungle, interspersed in summer with blooms of roses and tall colourful lupins. It had trees that cried out to be climbed. Clambering down further into the darkness was a deep well that we were certain had no bottom, together with a dank, dark pond, wherein some monstrous dread lurked.

The Blue Lagoon

During the summer of 1957 and under the guidance of Ian 'Sherf' Sherfield, we had all been making various improvements to our bicycle collective. Old, discarded mudguards were straightened and painted, saddlebags of various sizes were sourced, lights and reflectors fitted. I even had the forks on my old Hercules Artisan frame straightened. The objective of all this industry was to ensure that we were able to cycle around the island during the coming weeks.

The plan was, said Sherf, to choose a different area or town each day, spend some time there and cycle home by early evening, then start afresh the next morning, heading for a new venue. We would do this until we all had enough ability and fitness to undertake the round the island tour. Requirements were to be sandwiches and drinks (mainly water), as much money as we could beg, cozzies and towels. Being Island Boys, we were tousled-haired and as sun-kissed as the cornfields; we had no need of sun cream protection, but we all desired to wear cheap silver St. Christopher chains and the 'aviator look' with stylish new wire-framed polaroid sunglasses from Woolworths in Cowes.

A bicycle ride with my friends once took me to Sandown, a small coastal town on the eastern southern flank of the island. Sandown was always a favourite with holiday makers but not necessarily islanders, particularly those like me from the north of the Isle. Although the beaches were miles of uninterrupted golden sand and the shimmering sea was safe for swimmers to use, it could not match the sting and spray of the Solent. There was of course Punch and Judy and endless entertainment to be had at the theatre on the end of the pier, not to mention the scenic views in one direction across to Culver and down and across toward Shanklin. The panorama was wondrous.

As always on a bank holiday or when the weather was fine and warm, the beach was a noisy throng of garishly coloured sunhats, green canvas deckchairs and windbreaks. There would be an endless stream of braying donkeys wearily treading the water's edge, laden with children, and the sounds of hundreds of excited youngsters dressed in their rubber rings braving the gentle breakers. All with the sweet, sticky smell of candyfloss, ice cream and a distant but distinct scent of fried onions.

We were seeking out a lido, a swimming pool known locally as the Blue Lagoon. The Blue Lagoon, by scant repute, had the highest diving board on the island – or so Mike Brinton's Father had told him. We were all used, well able and competent enough to dive into the sea from the jetties, breakwaters or pontoons. There was, however, one very other important issue remaining to be discussed, debated or thought through. The plain fact of the matter was that not one of us had ever dived from a high springboard. It was an acrobatic skill thus far unknown and untried by any of us. But we comforted ourselves in the fact that we were Island Boys and nothing was insurmountable.

Once we had reached the Blue Lagoon all of us expressed surprise that it was a rooftop pool. We hurriedly paid nine pence to a plump lady at the window and ran upstairs to find tired, dirty changing stalls. Then, one by one, we appeared, shivering, at the pool's edge, looking into the murky, ice-cold water. Aghast, we craned our necks up and up at the high diving board.

There followed howls of derision and expletives as the varying views of our huddled band of brothers were expressed. Scathing opinions firstly regarding the less than blue of the icy cold Blue Lagoon and latterly the dizzying seven-metre-high diving platform stretching skyward before us.

'Bugger that for a lark,' cried Hicks defiantly, shading his eyes with his hand as he looked up. 'It doesn't look bloody safe to me.' He pointed to the high board and whispered hoarsely: 'Look, the whole bloody thing is wobbling!'

What followed was a very loud and robust discussion regarding the merits of both the pool and the diving board. We reasoned that, as Island Boys, we were all instinctive sons of the sea and as such this was a foolish and unsafe enterprise built for holiday makers and the like.

The noisy debacle was interrupted by the sudden appearance of a group of laughing girls making their entrance from the stairwell. Each was draped in large, brightly coloured bath towels and even brighter coloured bathing hats. Chatting noisily, they sat in a line upon the narrow wooden benching that ran down one side of the pool area. The last two to enter from the stairwell were two older women, both fully dressed and carrying gingham covered baskets. The taller of the two women waved and called out to us to ask if we had finished using the diving board. Her French accent was immediately noticeable and we nodded our collective agreeance back in as much a French manner as we could muster. To which, smiling broadly, she nodded back.

The other woman, leaning forward on her seat, cupped her hands to her mouth and shouted, 'Merci, merci les garçons, merci beaucoup.' She whispered briefly to the pretty girl on her immediate left, who stood up, facing us for a moment before turning smartly toward the diving board. She wore a black swimsuit and a bright yellow cap and the woman spoke loudly to her ensuring all the girls heard and paid attention.

'Simone, montre-nous toute ta belle plongée d'hirondelle dans l'eau, avec deux tours et un tour, s'il te plaît.'

The girl nodded and began climbing the steps until she reached the top of the board. Slowly, like a ballet dancer, she approached the end of the springing board. Holding her position for a moment before bouncing gracefully up into the air, she arched into her dive, her open arms coming together. Both of her legs were together as one as her body turned and turned again, slipping almost silently into the water. Within seconds the girl bobbed up on the far side of the pool, swimming for the ascent steps as her small group of companions clapped and shouted polite encouragement.

All of us stood thunderstruck as girl after girl performed a series of astonishing acrobatic dives into the pool, some diving backwards from the board. We looked on astounded and soon we found ourselves clapping and cheering and applauding the wonderful spectacle. The group of girls waiting their second chance of a dive waved and bobbed bows of appreciation.

The woman who spoke English was laughing and thoroughly enjoying the extravaganza of diving skills from her charges. She looked up and shouted across to us in her pretty French accent.

'We are so sorry for taking up so much time on the diving board, please you have been so patient to wait. Please to come' – she turned and gestured to the girls – 'show us girls how it should be done... how you say, um, how to do it properly... *n'est-ce pas.*'

At which point the girls as one squealed their delight, clapping their hands in loud approval and encouragement.

Her words hung over us like the glinting sword of Damocles. Our eyes had widened further than our open mouths, which were now hanging agape.

'And after, um, your diving...' continued the lady, searching for the right words, 'you are to, um... join us for some' – she paused, searching again – 'how you say, *rafraîchissements.*'

After a short while the group of girls began to point at us, unable to control or stifle their giggles. Their continued tittering was hushed by the two ladies, who were now opening the picnic baskets.

The excruciating sound of silent embarrassment was audible. It fell across our small group liken to stricken souls awaiting to cross the river Styx.

Suddenly, the tubby figure of Mike Brinton broke ranks, pushing us aside and exploding towards the pool, jumping high into the air with his knees tucked beneath his chin. Shouting *Geronimo!* he divebombed into the centre, disappearing into a massive plume of water. Then followed a splashing wave which covered very nearly everyone present, with a bobbing Brinton splashing out to the steps, much to the delight of the girls who were whooping and cheering loudly.

We were not to worry, as the girls and the two ladies found Mike's aquatic antics hilarious and we were all invited by the group to share their apples, pâté and cheese.

The fact that not one of us was able to communicate and explain exactly the reticence for our lack of diving skills was due entirely to our inability to speak or understand French.

Osborne Bay Beach

"It is impossible to imagine a prettier spot."
— Queen Victoria, speaking of Osborne House

Into the roll me down roll me over
Waiting for the tide
Into folds of salt and stinging
Down into the long lost gentle rhythms
Lost forever where no one can find me out
Tangled cadence of liquid after music
The sea

Pulsing to the anywhere of the music
Leaving where I need to be
Swimming in the warm long song
Riding me upon curling salt-crested waves
Rocking rolling
High upon shingle shells a green glass sea
Splashing emeralds over tip and toe
The shore

Whitecroft Hospital

My Mother had been transferred to Whitecroft, a hospital at Gatcombe a mile or so outside the island's capital town of Newport. The staff there, my Grandmother had said, were better able and better equipped to deal with her peculiar illness. Her general health and mental condition were undoubtedly deteriorating, made worse, my Grandmother had insisted, by constant medication and sedation.

The consequent quashing and restriction of any thought process by the patient was for the orderly convenience of the irascible guardians, who squeaked up and down the long dark corridors in starched white uniforms like bullies off to school.

'Pills, pills and more pills,' hissed my Grandmother.

'All the pills in the world won't get rid of her Voices,' I whispered.

I was right.

One day, as I watched my Mother being helped to the toilet by one of the nursing staff, I noticed her tiny frail hand reach out and tap the door handle at least four times before entering. Sometimes when sitting up, my Mother would dust her water tumbler with a clean handkerchief for the whole hour we sat there. Often, she would be seen scrubbing her slippers in the handbasin before venturing back down the ward, her feet and slippers soaked through.

When we returned home my Grandmother would go to the kitchen to make supper, then sit in her armchair. I would sit crossed-legged upon the rag mat in front of the shining black range that glowed red and smelt of soup. We would listen to the crackle of the radio until it was time for me to go to bed, leaving her to her snuff box and the ten o'clock news.

Pulling the blankets and eiderdown tight about me in the chilly darkness, my thoughts would turn to the day's events and then to my 'Aunt', Shirley. I would imagine that I was staying in the glow of the cheery embers of her fireside, dreaming that we were chatting over steaming mugs of cocoa and a secret cigarette. Then Shirley would call it a night and retire to the sun, moon and stars of her bedroom, leaving me to contemplate the wonder of it all in the dancing firelight of my fantasy.

As I lay in the cold sepia of the musty back bedroom at Gran's, I could sense that somehow Shirley knew that I was thinking of her. I was sure she knew and that she was very close by. A feeling as intense as it was strange, but safe and comforting.

Night and dream come spinning downy-soft all about me. Soft, feathering stars all about me, dancing.

'Night Shirley.'
'God bless, Gus.'

Time for Tea

A lonely place a Sunday
Down a climb and rocky shoreline
Down a climb and sandy shingle
Where you can see the far edge of somewhere
Where the far edge can see you clearly
It's nearly time for tea

A lonely place a Sunday
Down a climb and tides for ebbing
Down a climb and stone lion roaring
Where you can see the white horses flying
Where the white horses can see you clearly
It's nearly time for tea

A lonely place a Sunday
Down a climb wind and stinging
Down a climb buoys and breakwater
Where you can see west across the Medina
When the Medina knows you're there
Where you can see the white horses flying
Where you can see the far edge of somewhere
Where the green sea Solent sees you clearly
It's nearly time for tea

Maria and Her Mother

By the summer of 1954, my Mother had been finally released from hospital and we were staying for a short while at my Grandmother's house in Moorgreen Road, West Cowes. We had been there just over a fortnight and there had been no sign or visitations from her Voices. All in all, she was in high spirits and seemed much happier and self-assured. Mary and Margaret, two of the young girls from next door, had called round to see her, bringing homemade cakes and flowers from their garden. Things seemed to be much improved.

After breakfast my Grandmother gave me a pencilled list.

'Nip up to Jim Maughan's dear and get a few things... and be bloody careful with them eggs.'

A large, shining, maroon Humber Sceptre motor car was parked right outside Mr Maughan's small corner greengrocery shop, its engine still running. Inside this luxurious car, standing defiantly on its hind legs, was a small white dog, yapping and scratching at the window. I examined and drank in as much of this beautiful car as I could whilst the dog within grew evermore apoplectic with rage.

'Nice having your Mum back I expect,' trilled Mr Maughan in his usual whistling hiss. 'Now then, half of cooked ham...'

He continued to complete my Grandmother's list in a distant, shrilling monotone, his words whispering out of the open widow as he moved, list in hand, from shelf to shelf.

My attention had now been taken by quite the prettiest girl I had ever seen. Her eyes, wide and dark as mystery, flashed and sparkled like Benzie's window at Christmas. I took the time and opportunity to smile at her and expected a response.

There was none.

'Well, as soon as we finish up here, Maria and I are going to Newport to shop before returning to East Cowes.'

The voice belonged to a woman who was being served by Mrs Maughan. It was high and scratchy, pretentiously extending and pronouncing her words oddly, whilst dismissing her conversation with whisking, affected hand movements.

'My husband has taken up a commission in Germany pro tem, whilst we, alas, are forced to linger here on the island in East Cowes for the summer.'

'Germany... Oh I say, East Cowes. Whereabouts in East—'

'And a tin of peas,' interjected the woman. 'Petit pois.'

Her demand hung in the air.

Both Mr and Mrs Maughan looked at her askance.

Moments later, in a perfumed flounce and tinkle of the shop door, Maria and her Mother were gone.

'Bloody overners,' piped Mr Maughan through his teeth.

'Lady bloody Muck more like, if you ask me,' tutted Mrs Maughan, clearly unimpressed.

My mind was in a whirl.

Mary, Margaret and Marilyn

Mary, Margaret and Marilyn
We played at doctors in the shed
They covered me in plasters
Tied crepe bandage to my head

Mary, Margaret and Marilyn
We played at cowboys in the shed
They shot me full of bullets
They filled me full of lead

Mary, Margaret and Marilyn
We played at nurses in the shed
They wrapped me in cotton sheets
Then they tied me to the bed

Mary, Margaret and Marilyn
We played at vicars in the shed
They covered me up in flowers
Then they pretended I was dead

The Sketchbook

My Mother and Father had made strident efforts at various times over the years to make a lasting partnership, but such was the island's local stigma and prudency that they were immediately seen as outsiders by both families and friends.

I recall my Mother once wearing a beautiful, bright red, full silk skirt and soft knitted white bolero. With her long, black, curly hair wisping all ways, she took my Father's arm before alighting down the grim, cold staircase in Kent House. Eyes bright and wide, he was smiling broadly at her, his naturally wavy golden hair slicked flat by brilliantine. Smelling of mothballs and cheap cologne, my Father was dressed in his light grey James Cagney suit, sporting a wide garish tie you would not wear for a dare.

In my hands was my sketchbook, my pencil busy outlining the view of the front entrance of Kent House from where my Mother and Father had just emerged.

'Going for a walk. Won't be long, bring you something nice back,' shouted my Mother, waving a white gloved hand in my direction.

'Mind you don't fall out of that bloody tree nipper,' I heard my Father shout back, as they rounded the short path that led to York Avenue.

From my position in the tree, I shrugged a reply as I watched them disappear into the pink evening light.

One of my delights was drawing. Not so much pen and ink or painting – heaven forbid that the pallid thin watercolours might stain or leave a permanent reminder of creativity in their wake.

The Voices demanded order as well as cleanliness.

And so, my art was mainly the pencil variety, usually on the yellowing back flyleaf paper removed from library or textbooks. Imagine my delight following a visit to Shirley's, when she gave me a sketchbook and a box of coloured pencils! Drawing, together with the help of my imagination, afforded not so much an escape as another comfortable hiding place. I vowed to carry the sketchbook and pencils with me wherever I went. Throughout the rest of that summer of 1954 the world was there, it seemed, for my delight to record.

It was such an occasion, a day or two later, that I was interrupted as I lay huddled beside the rocks on Gurnard beach, cheating the cutting wind as it skimmed in from the Solent. Close by, in the damp sand, was a group of young girls in thin, pretty, cotton dresses with bright ribbons and their pigtails flying. They were chanting a singsong skipping game. Taking up my pencils, I scribbled their laughter and vitality busily into my sketchbook.

'Bugger me, I think I've seen everything now!'

This rude intrusion was from my once constant 'Tree Camp' companion, Alan Hick, laughing loudly as he called over his shoulder. A little further down the beach, struggling with something at the water's edge, was Mike Brinton.

Alan waved his arm wildly.

'Come here Mike, come and see what the tide's washed up.'

Mike, who had been pulling a large piece of driftwood behind him, ran up the beach. Grinning widely, he craned over my shoulder.

'Wotcher Gus, we haven't seen you for ages nipper.'

'I've been staying—'

'What's it supposed to be then?' he interjected, jabbing at my open sketchbook and showering the page with shingle from his grubby wet finger.

'Girls skipping,' I heard myself saying in a monotone.

'You want to give it a rest, our young'un can do better than that.'

'Yeah and he's only four,' shrieked Alan.

His convulsions were suddenly cut short by him slipping between the seaweed-strewn green rocks into a shallow rock pool. After an explosion of expletives, a flailing arm was seen.

'Give us a bloody hand up then!' he shouted. 'Bugger! I'm bloody soaking. Look, I'm bleeding.'

He waved his scraped hand in the air to shake out the pain, whistle-hissing through his teeth. Mike proffered both a helping hand and a ragged handkerchief.

'You must be bloody joking! Christ only knows where you've had that thing,' howled Alan, thrusting his bleeding hand deep into his pocket for comfort.

'When did you take up drawing then?' asked Mike.

'Been doing it for ages,' I shrugged.

'Let's see what else you've done,' asked Alan.

'You can when I've finished,' I said, watching the two eldest girls dancing into the turning rope.

...*In came a bogeyman and pushed me out!*

'Your Mum's up the hospital, isn't she? Is she ill then?' said Mike, holding his flapping, raggy handkerchief aloft between outstretched fingers.

'Is she up St. Mary's Hospital?' asked Alan.

I nodded, pretending to be far more interested in my drawing of the girls than updating Alan, who would certainly be in his Mother's good books if he was able to bring fresh gossip home.

'Our Mum says that you must probably be over West at your Gran's house.'

My head stayed in my book.

'So, me and Mike called at your Gran's this morning and she said you was over East staying with your Dad,' shrugged Alan. 'So, me an' Mike says, let's go over to Gurnard for a bit of laugh on the shore and then bugger me, guess who we find?'

'Yeah, that's really queer mate,' said Mike. 'Especially when your Dad thought you was over West with your Gran.'

'So, where you been and why are you over here?' posed the jabbing, pointed finger of Alan.

Their undoing words hung like knives in the air. Hardly audible, my rasping whisper was awaited by the two expectant boys.

'I been staying with one of my Aunties.'

Down came a blackbird and pecked off her snout...

'One of your Aunties!' repeated an incredulous Alan.

'What Auntie is that then?' asked Mike softly, as he busied himself with filling his handkerchief with soft, sandy shingle.

'Be his daft old Aunt Min,' laughed Alan.

'Who?'

'You know,' said Alan, attempting a grotesque impression of poor Aunt Min. 'Her that gets drunk down at The Commercial over Cowes every Saturday night.'

'Then pisses her pants,' laughed Mike inanely.

'Bugger off!' I bellowed. 'If you must know, old Aunt Min lives with my Gran over West!'

She flew to the window...

All my loud protests were for nothing. They were met with nothing but hoots of derision and increased enquiry concerning the whereabouts of my mysterious Aunt.

'I've got loads of Aunts over here,' I said without looking up.

'Where?' asked Mike in a loud doubting tone.

'Yeah, where does she live?' sneered Alan.

Gesturing, I waved my arm in the direction of the Gurnard marshes which ran close to the shoreline.

'Over there somewhere,' I said. 'Not far.'

What a pretty view, whatever shall I do…

'What's her name then? Auntie who?' yelled Mike, as he leaned back and began to spin the ragged sling of shingle above his head faster and faster.

'Shirley…'

Both boys pretended not to hear, but neither would dare to forget before they got back home to divulge this snippet of gossip to their Mothers.

'Where is she then? This Auntie of yours…'

'She gone up Newport in her car. It's a Ford Prefect.'

As I uttered the words *car* and *Ford Prefect*, both boys' bright eyes widened and their mouths fell agape.

…then up came a bogeyman and threw her OUT!

The girls screamed and scattered as the handkerchief full of shingle burst in their midst, leaving Alan Hick and Mike Brinton spinning in the sand helpless with laughter.

After a short altercation with the parents of one of the girls, we moved off down the shoreline in the general direction of Cowes.

We walked and talked until finally Egypt Point loomed into view, by which time I had furnished the boys with most of the details concerning my poor Mother's decline and most of the recent changes and happenings to my life. And always careful to mention Shirley in the guise of a long-lost Auntie who had elected to take care of me overnight, before returning to Gran's whilst my Mother recovered from her illness.

Parting company was noisy and boisterous, as my two friends continued to shout crude obscenities at each other as they raced up the steep stone steps that led up from the beach to the Coast Road and back to the small town of West Cowes.

Beneath the Tree

Beneath the tree where Prince stands quietly
Beside the cold round iron fence
Beside the flowering stinging nettles
Tall reeds and bramble twine

Beneath the tree where Prince stands quietly
Beside the brown cow gently lowing
Beside the sow and squealing piglet
Stands a boy in brightest summer
Stands a boy, his hair is golden

Beside the hedgerow and the thicket
Beneath the tree where Prince stands quietly
Came then autumn
Came winter too
Beneath the tree

Prince was a gentle giant, an almost permanent feature of my boyhood. A large bay Shire horse who, when not stood gazing at us at play, grazed quietly and serenely upon the fields between East Cowes Castle and York Avenue.

Going Home

It had been almost a month, as joyous and as happy as I can ever remember a month ever being. Gran, Uncle Donald and old Aunt Min all enjoying the return to rude health of my almost radiant Mother. Every moment was wonderful. Every day carefree and happy. Finally, my Mother had decided that after such a long stay it was high time for us to cross the river and return to our home in East Cowes.

Our walk from West Cowes to East Cowes involved my Mother being stopped by many local ladies, all of whom were desperate for an exclusive update on her wellbeing. I listened to her lies and dithering from one subject to the next, whilst the well-meaning ladies of the parish, eyes narrowing and unblinking, their expressions in pinched consternation, listened in coerced empathy. The whipping estuary wind and the loud grinding of the heavy chains on the short ferry crossing helped drown out yet more well-wishers.

Once over to East Cowes my Mother busied her way from the chain ferry to the Spurs Café on Clarence Road, where I had been promised a cheese roll and a milkshake. We sat close to the far counter beside the kitchen, whereupon Mrs Maskell fell upon my Mother, smothering her with kisses and hugs, both women enraptured in their joyful reunion. Soon Mr Maskell and the staff of the café were crowding excitedly around my Mother in the small annexed area beside the counter.

The jangle of the entrance door sounded, followed by a loud clattering of seats being pulled across the linoleum floor into position.

'Hello… Hello?' insisted a voice, calling high and loud. 'If it's not too much trouble, can I have a menu? Maria darling, can you see if there is a speciality board anywhere?'

I turned from my seat in the outer annex to see the front of the small café darkened by the shadow of a huge motor car – a Humber Sceptre – which was parked immediately in front of the small entrance.

Seated at one of the pastel-coloured metal bistro tables was a Mother and her very pretty daughter.

An immediate flurry of activity surrounded the pair as sweet Molly Fry attended to their requests for refreshments. Demands could be heard clearly in every sharp and flat, whilst flaying hands and dramatic gestures reinforced her urgency. The last requirement was to bring a cold glass of *lemon-ard* and to be sure to place within it a scoop of *von-illa* ice cream, together with two straws. Evidently it was Maria's favourite.

As all this was taking place, Mrs Maskell was huddled with my Mother in a muffled giggle, liken to two naughty schoolgirls.

'Here, make yourself useful,' said Mr Maskell, nodding in the general direction of the two seated customers. With that, he thrust a small plastic tray into my hands, upon which, perilously balanced, were a tea pot, milk, sugar and plates. He winked and imitating in *la dee dah* as best he could, added: 'Tell 'em young Molly will be through in a jiffy with the *von-illa* ice cream and *lemon-ard*.'

I very carefully wobbled the tray to a standstill upon their table, smiling broadly into the pretty face of Maria, who smiled across at me in return.

'Thank you,' she whispered.

For the second time in as many days, my mind was in a whirl.

Half an hour later we were walking up the stony drive to the entrance of our home, a small flat, within the fading grandeur of Kent House on York Avenue. As my Mother turned the key slowly in the door, she suddenly took a sharp intake of breath. Then, gasping, she stood leaning against the door for a moment to stem an almost uncontrollable shaking. She clutched her breast as though she had been stabbed through the heart, eyes closed tight, her face contorted as though in pain, her mouth opened in a loud silent scream.

It was as though someone had flicked a switch. In an instant she was no longer my pretty, happy Mother, she had become instead a desperate and instantly terrified woman who had returned to being at the mercy of those wicked and vindictive Voices. The Voices which still dwelt here within our home in Kent House. The Voices that had patiently lain in wait like avenging angels expecting her eventual return.

Shaking and trembling, she entered the small flat, slamming the door hard behind her. I heard the key turn loudly in the lock and she was gone, leaving me and my small brown suitcase outside upon the doormat. After a moment or two I heard her sobbing and crying out to some entity.

I knew from experience it could be a long, long wait.

Hours later, the front door eventually opened, bidding me enter to the odious stench of disinfectant.

The Lady on York Avenue

The bitter tingle smell of bay leaf after the rain
White roses rolling tangled over the arch
That leads up to the terrace stones dancing always
Cracked tiles over the patio beneath the flowering thistle

She, much older now, so much older
White stone smothered pink and yellow with lichen
Paintwork flaked blows away on the wind
Her flowerbeds returned to seed
Lie neglected beneath a rusting car

She cannot hear the river shipyards now
Or the patter of excited boys running amok
Down in her cellars or high up in her attics
Comforted as ever by the bell of the Town Hall
Measuring time and memories a-more

A majestic French oak standing alone
Beside a hamlet of small homes cover the quiet orchards
The dark fishing lake and well long since dry
Tranquil fading elegance broken by time

The Table

I was awoken by thunderous knocking. Muffled voices were at the front door.

It was the summer of 1956, an early Sunday morning, and I could soon make out my Mother's voice, together with those belonging to my Father and his younger brother Roy.

'You said you were coming sometime next week,' said Mother.

'Roy's busy next week over the mainland and I need him to help me get it down the stairs and out onto the front,' explained my Father.

He was referring to the large, white, scrubbed pine table that served as a dining table in the small front room of our flat. The large pine table had seen better days and had of late developed a wobble due to a loose leg. It was urgently in need of some attention or repair.

My Mother carefully cleared the table and almost immediately began issuing a stream of instructions to my Father and Uncle as to how the table should be lifted and thereafter carefully manoeuvred down the turning staircase to the entrance hallway.

Once outside, the heavy table was manhandled through the overgrown rose arch and out into the open walled terrace area so my Father and Roy could begin its repair. The two small cutlery drawers were removed to be varnished, whilst the loose leg was attended to. It was past midday on a very warm summer's day and Roy, mopping his brow, suggested that they should return later to varnish the table.

'The bugger will be safe enough here 'til tomorrow,' he declared.

'Tomorrow,' repeated my Father, nodding an enthusiastic agreement. 'Yeah, you're right nipper. Besides, I could murder a bloody pint.'

They walked together down York Avenue, laughing as they crossed The Rec. They were still wiping their brows when they entered the Victoria Tavern on Clarence Road.

They checked the time.

'A couple of hours won't hurt,' said Roy.

The following Thursday afternoon, the table was still standing smartly to attention on the terrace where my Father and Roy had left it. The two small drawers stacked beside it were now full of rainwater. My Mother's fury and frustration had been spent and she, like me, assumed that both Roy and my Father would return this coming weekend.

'What's going on with your table?' asked Robert Mullet. 'It's been outside for days.'

Robert lived in a small flat beneath ours in Kent House. We had been friends for many years, albeit he attended a different school to the rest of us – the Technical School on Osborne Road.

'Are you slinging it out then? Could be chopped for firewood,' he suggested, his sensible practicality shining through, before rambling on. 'Pity we haven't got a shed, could be useful as a workbench.'

I spent the next five minutes explaining the situation to him as we walked the short distance together down York Avenue to the bungalow where our mutual friend Sherf lived.

The three of us were soon over the road making our way through the shrubby bushes and into Bommy Building. Sherf seemed preoccupied and began busying himself, scanning the upper reaches of the surrounding trees. It was not too long before he had climbed up into one. The tree that he had climbed into was approximately thirty feet tall and the main trunk split into four or more branches. It resembled an open hand with the cupped fingers upstretched.

'Fancy building a tree camp?' he asked, as he swung down

from the tree into a crash of leaves and twigs that formed the deep undergrowth.

During the past couple of years, we had built many camps, some more sophisticated and permanent than others. There had been an underground camp, which really had been no more than a deep trench covered by corrugated metal sheets and lined with sacking. We had also built various bush branches and foliage-covered bivouacs with entrances and ground seating lined with straw and leaves. Many of these camps had been discovered by parents worried about the hazards of campfires, or by other boys who delighted in destroying our gang camp. However, this camp, explained Sherf, was to be vastly different. It was going to be built thirty feet from the ground into the canopy of a tree and (in his opinion) almost impossible to find.

Soon we had rallied some other friends – Mike Brinton, Alan Hick and Dave Elliot – and whilst Sherf was the architect of the undertaking he was also the taskmaster. He soon had us all lopping and chopping, sawing and hammering his plan into place. Meanwhile, he had obtained nails, a saw, ropes and a hammer, and was busy constructing a crude pulley. The pulley system enabled us to transfer pieces of wood and asbestos sheeting to those of us in the tree, whereupon we would lash or affix a framework which functioned as a stout and sturdy wall nailed to branches. Over the next week or so, we begged and borrowed every bit of spare lumber we could find. The camp was almost complete, its walls were built and there was also a window of sorts and a very adequate roof and entrance. We had even fashioned a short rope ladder by which we were able to make easier access, albeit after climbing the initial twenty-five feet or so branch by branch. The only fly in the ointment was the lack of an adequate floor or base: due to the nature of the tree, there was no flat surface, just the jutting stubs of the recently cut boughs. The wind was also a consideration insofar as we did not have corners as such to enable us to lash the side walls tight enough to ensure they were weathertight; they were only timber boards covered over by old pieces of tarpaulin and mineral felt.

"'Ere, Gus, I've had an idea,' said Sherf suddenly, shaking me by the shoulders and staring earnestly into my face. 'What about your Dad's old table? It's been out the front of your place for bloody weeks. I'm sure your Dad has forgotten about the bugger.'

Sherf's eyes grew wide and bright as he excitedly explained and outlined his plans to us all.

'Don't you see, if we had it, if we took that old table, we could hoist the bloody thing up to the top, the underside of the tabletop would be the floor and we could use the legs as corner posts to lash and tighten everything so the bloody wind doesn't get in and under.'

We all stood in absolute silence, mouths agape, as we listened. The realisation of what had just been suggested was sinking in.

The premise was: steal my Father's table, hoist it thirty feet up a tree, use it as the tree camp floor and main structure, and notwithstanding, undertake this outrageous theft in broad daylight.

Sherf convinced us all that the effrontery of such a theft was in itself the key to its success – in the unlikely event we were seen it would naturally be accepted that we boys were simply moving Gus's Dad's table as an errand or task. As the table was positioned directly beneath the projecting bay window of the flat where I lived and completely out of view of my Mother, and it would be doubtful that she would be looking out of the high window anyway, the plan was accepted by all as plausible.

The legs of the table were the first items to be removed. They were affixed beneath the table by butterfly-nuts in each corner. We quickly made the short journey from Kent House to the trees that edged the fields of Bommy Building, carrying the stout table legs under our arms.

Ten minutes later we had returned to carry the tabletop. The six-foot by four-foot slab of thick pine was heavy and resulted in several accidental drops as we all weaved our gasping and grunting way back to the base of the intended tree.

This audacious theft was accomplished with no questioning or sight of us ever being reported. The theft of the table had been a complete and utter success.

'Told ya,' said Sherf, smirking and puffing out his chest. 'No one will ever know it was us.'

The table was truly the answer to the stability and success and eventual longevity of our tree camp, but for now it was complete as it gently swayed high and hidden in the trees above. Prince, the golden Shire horse, the only spectator from the field below.

The days and weeks immediately following were however somewhat more stressful, particularly for my Father, who searched the area and questioned all and sundry about the missing table.

'A bloody queer carry on altogether if you ask me,' said my Father, pulling his hand through his hair in exasperation. 'I don't understand why the buggers left the bloody drawers behind.'

'Probably chopped the bugger up for firewood, more like.' my Mother exclaimed, rolling her eyes to the heavens. 'T'was all it was fit for. Bloody thing wobbled anyway, wasn't safe. It needed to be replaced.'

Their difference of opinions upon the virtues of their table wisped up into the warm evening air, their words spiralling high into the summer sky, alighting as a gentle rustling deep within the canopy of the tree. Wherein four boys, their happy faces lit by candlelight, sat smoking Woodbines.

Long Ago, When We Were Nippers

In the top field beside the tall grass
Long ago, when we were nippers
Hidden by the green grass bushes
Hidden so no one else could see
Beneath the trees we built a cabin
Built of logs and broken branches
Logs and twig leaf built by nippers
In the top field beside the tall grass
Long ago, when we were nippers

In the top field beside the tall grass
We dug the earth with spade and spit
Beneath the ground we dug a tunnel
Long ago, when we were nippers
Tunnelled beneath the scented bay
Beside the spruce and mountain ash
Beneath the rambling rose and laurel
Beneath the clay and coiling root
Long ago, when we were nippers

High in a sycamore we built a tree camp
With climbing holds to find our way
With an upturned table for a floor
We built a tree camp hidden by twig leaf
Hidden so no one else could see
Long ago, when we were nippers
Within all was warm and bright with candle
Hidden from the world above the tall grass
Hidden so no one else could see
Long ago, when we were nippers

The Mystery Tour

Auntie Min and Uncle Don lived as lodgers at my Grandmother's in Moorgreen Road. I recall an occasion in 1955 when, as a special treat, they took me on a mystery tour one evening in a charabanc. I remember being very excited as we climbed into this beautiful shining cream and green vehicle. After we had all boarded, and although Auntie Min was sat chain-smoking cigarettes beside me, I was allowed the window seat. The charabanc picked us up from opposite The Westwood sports ground in Park Road in West Cowes, but unfortunately not long after we had set off it began to rain – a dark stormy squall blowing across the island from the Solent. I remember being so disappointed.

I was told later by my Auntie Min that by the time we were passing through Newport I had fallen sound asleep. I had not even wakened when we had reached our intended destination, our rendezvous with 'mystery'. Evidently, this mystery tour was bound for a small village at the southerly tip of the island called Niton and the warm and welcoming hospitality of the famous Buddle Inn. Although I discovered this later, it came as no surprise to me that a convivial evening was being enjoyed by all.

All, that is, except myself and another child, a little girl whose name was Myra. She was not very pretty and had difficulty in speaking coherently due to her suffering the disability of a cleft palette. This gave her a massive overbite; so much so, she took on a beaver-like resemblance. We both sat there together for the next two hours playing I Spy, which with Myra's speech impediment made the long evening all the more surreal. Occasionally the door at the front of the charabanc would slide open with a bang and a cheery soul, beaming from ear to ear, would bring us crisps, cheese rolls and bottles of American Cream Soda.

The mystery tour had been organised some time ago by members of the social committee from my Uncle's pub, The Commercial Inn in Cowes High Street. Amazingly, the coach driver who was enjoying the evening and imbibing with the rest of the gathering was the landlord himself.

I have vivid recollections of a very noisy and boisterous return journey to West Cowes.

We followed each other from the charabanc back into the The Commercial Inn. It was still raining heavily, the raindrops running like tears down the patterned glass of the saloon bar.

It was well into the early hours of the next morning when my Auntie and Uncle both finally decided to leave. They wove from one side of the pavement to the next as they struggled back in the pouring rain, arms linked, singing tuneless and inane songs at the top of their voices. I all too well remember the sorry yet comical sight of them in a slow and tedious progress towards Moorgreen Road, celebrating the fruits of a what they told me was a 'Lock In'.

Raining on the Beach

November's blowing
It is starting to rain again
Running down my face again
Grey lace hiding the mainland
My smile stolen, carried out to sea
A ragged shingle edge
Stinging my hands
Blood and salt
Ringing loud and clear
Shells singing in my ear
Wild white horses prancing
Dancing all ways ever
So far away
So long ago

Knowledge

Early every Sunday morning, on my way to carry out my labour of love for Tic's birds (which was to dig and fill small sacks of shingle from the beach at East Cowes), I would stop to press my nose against Mr French's bicycle shop window and dream.

Due to the lack of money, generally very few of my friends were being bought these amazing machines. Those that had acquired them won additional admiration for sporting and discussing in matter-of-fact terms to one another the 'knowledge'. Knowledge that separated the discerning from those that could only dream and envy.

The knowledge was the wherewithal to discuss and compare with ease the lightweight, handmade frames from manufacturers named Jack Taylor, Holdsworth and Claud Butler. The broad plethora of this elitist knowledge also included an array of bicycle speak, such as the various selection of Deralia gears available, dropped handlebars, fixed gear wheels, sport drinking bottle holders, rat trap and caged racing pedals, and leather racing saddles that were as thin as pencils.

On rare occasions, one of my fortunate friends would offer me a trial or try out on his marvellous machine. I had always declined. Although I could do the bicycle speak quite convincingly, no one knew my deeply held secret that I held clasped to my beating breast: I had never learned to ride a bike.

One warm, stormy late summer evening, when the air was heavy and sweet with the smell of russet apple, plum and pear, I was sat in the long cool grass watching my Father. He was attempting to ride my Grandma Hilda's old bicycle down Tic's garden, the wicker basket on the front filled to the brim with gooseberries. They were spilling out like green bullets in all directions as he sped, bumping and wobbling his way, down the narrow garden path. He cut a very comic figure, his long legs splayed out wide each side of the little black bike as he slid to a dusty stop beside Tic's shed. As I helped my Father tip the gooseberries into a large, chipped enamel bowl ready for Grandma Hilda to make jam, the conversation turned to that of bicycles.

It was growing dark before we had finished talking, my Father crunching through apple after apple as I expounded the advantages of owning a bicycle, outlining the pros and cons of the various types, styles and manufacturers. I had never enjoyed an evening with my Father as much as on that balmy summer's evening – not that there had been many. Although I was sure that I had convinced him that I had a broad and confident knowledge of bicycles, I did not divulge my secret to him.

No Matter Sunday Morning

No matter Sunday morning
Melting away
All against the shingle's salty edge
The swan early jackdaw crack of day
Pocket deep sting
The ring jingle of being stony broke
Like the seawater in my shoes
I had nothing to lose but the words
As they drift from one dream to the next
To be thrown up upon some other shore
Perplexed and broken
Comes the squalling wind that steals
Scattering my words to the everywhere
Amber beads and silver seashells
Amber beads and lucky stones

The summer of 1954 became a distant memory as autumn gave way to the chill of winter, heralding the fact that the festive season was imminent. Midst the neat rows of boys in the choir stalls to the strains of 'Oh Holy Night', I silently prayed to God to gift me, in the event that he loved me and also for the fact that I was singing my heart out like an angel, a bicycle. Specifically, a super, splendid racer. It would be the envy of my peer group; a bicycle like no other.

Christmas through to New Year was always spent with my Mother, Aunties and Uncles at my Grandmother's in Moorgreen Road. The pungent smell of stored apple and floor polish filled the air of the rarely opened front room. Homemade paperchains bedecked the small room, made cosy by a bright coal fire blazing in the hearth.

The atmosphere was exciting and busy and my thoughts turned once again to that of a bicycle. Might there be one waiting, bright and chromed and French racing saddled? I had completely buried my inadequacy.

The family was in high spirits and acting, I felt, a little strangely.

Uncle Don kept winking at me with slow knowing nods.

'Wonder what Santa is going to be bringing you this year nip? Hope you've been good,' he chuckled, followed by another wink, itself followed by Auntie Min slapping him lightly and bidding him to hush.

'That's enough, you silly old bugger,' she gasped, coughing acrid clouds of Wild Woodbine in all directions.

Later, in the darkness of my small bedroom, the enchantment and the wonder of Christmas Eve magic and holiness spiralled all about me. I listened for as long as I could to the distant rattle from the kitchen, to merriment and laughter. Came then the long, dark, silent night, the holy night that is Christmas Eve, before dawn bade me awake to a Five Boys chocolate bar, a packet of white handkerchiefs and the smell of tangerine. At long last, Christmas morning had arrived.

An hour or so later, after fighting the desperate urge to fly down the stairs (which I knew was forbidden), I heard hushed whispers and then my name being called.

A greeting of *Merry Christmas* was being given by everyone to everyone. A breakfast of tea and toast was being taken by Uncles, whilst the ladies continued with the steaming labour of the Christmas dinner. The crackling radio in the corner of the back room was playing Christmas carols when my Grandmother suddenly looked up from preparing a tray of vegetables.

'It's time we all went to the front room and started Christmas,' she declared. Then, placing her hand on my shoulder, she whispered: 'And you, young man, should close your eyes till I tell you to open them.'

I was beside myself with excited anticipation. *Was this it?* My mind was spinning. Was this the moment that my dreams and prayers were to be answered?

Immediately, I did as I had been told. With my eyes shut tight, I could hear my Mother's voice, together with that of my Uncle Don and the rustling of paper.

'Careful, Don,' I heard her say.

'Bloody hell Brenda, I am being careful. The bugger's bloody heavy,' hissed Donald.

'Shush,' scolded my Grandmother. 'Right sweetheart, you can open your eyes now. Happy Christmas!'

The rejoinder of *Happy Christmas*, together with the loud smacking of kisses and exclamations of joy resounded from everyone. They echoed down the long, polished passage of the hallway, accompanied by giggles from both my Mother and Auntie Min.

'See my love, wishes do come true. What do you think of that, isn't it beautiful?'

Leaning against the wall of the passage was a bicycle.

There had been a meagre attempt at Christmas decoration and a sad silver string of tinsel looped around its crossbar. At first glance it took on the look of an abandoned errand boy's bike waiting to be packed with parcels and bread.

My heart sank.

My mouth was as dry as sand as I croaked my thanks to my gathered and jubilant family. I smiled as best I could to one and all and kissed my Mother with dusty parched lips.

I will never be completely sure if it was the large black saddlebag or the front-affixed woven cane shopping basket that first caught my eye. It may have been the large sensible bell or the white bicycle pump.

The bicycle was a black Hercules Artisan. Its actual pump had been mislaid in transit and Mr French at the bicycle shop had loaned Uncle Don the white one until it could be replaced in a week or two.

My Uncle had been correct when announcing earlier that the bike was heavy. It weighed a ton.

My imitation of giddy delight in front of my family passed muster. Everyone was overjoyed at my supposed pleasure to be, at long last, the proud owner of my very own bicycle.

Several days prior to Christmas Eve, my Father had arranged with Mr French to deliver the Hercules to my Grandmother's house to be sure it was there for Christmas morning. There was a message that he would like me to ride over on Boxing Day to East Cowes and visit him and show off my new bike to Tic and Grandmother Hilda.

Now here I was, aged eleven years old, unable to ride my Hercules Artisan and facing the prospect of embarrassment and ridicule once I had explained the fact to one and all that I was not able to ride the bike.

What a dilemma! A quandary of my own making. My stomach was a mass of dancing butterflies.

The morning progressed and the family exchange of gifts had taken place. I was now standing resplendent in my new Christmas jumper (a garish green, which has never suited me, but no matter – it was Christmas). I was also sporting a leather gun belt, silver six-shooter and holster, and a far too large black cowboy hat with gold tassels.

Christmas lunch had been served and my appetite was diminished so much so that I had declined Christmas pudding and the usual desperate search for sixpences.

My Grandmother was clearly worried, thinking I was ailing and coming down with some sort of seasonal cold or sniffle.

'Whatever's wrong sweetheart?'

'He hasn't looked at all well since he got up,' said my Mother.

'He's probably got something,' said Auntie Min, taking another sip of her brandy.

I stood up, sobbing, and blurted out my confession.

'I can't ride a bike,' I heard myself saying.

'What?' said Auntie Min. 'You've never been able to ride a bike? Well, they say you will never forget once you've learnt.'

'He can't ride a bike?' said Uncle Don and removed his glasses, shaking his head in disbelief. His words hung in the air. 'What does he mean, he can't ride a bike? Everyone can ride a bloody bike! Never heard of such a thing.'

My Grandmother and Mother were aghast, their mouths wide open in clear disbelief at what they had just heard.

'No such word as can't,' said Auntie Min, coughing loudly into another cigarette.

Finally, my Mother spoke, her tone one of annoyance.

'He does nothing but talk bikes when he comes back from his Father's. Well, I was sure his Father had taught him, for all the time he spends there.'

Shaking his head in bewilderment, my Uncle pointed out: 'Why on Earth would Stan buy him a bloody bike if he couldn't ride the bugger?'

Following much consternation and discussion, and having finished his second bottle of stout, he took me to one side.

'Tell you what nipper,' he suggested, 'tomorrow me and you are going to push your bike over to your Father's at East Cowes, just like he asked, and you're going to thank him for his Christmas present to you. But you're going to have to be honest and tell him you can't ride the bugger.'

'Yes indeed,' my Grandmother interjected. 'Your Father will need to teach you how to ride a bicycle!'

Sleeping was particularly difficult that Christmas night. Half-dreams and visions of sleek beautiful racing bikes filled my mind. I lay in the darkness, imagining the expressions on the faces of my Father and my cousins and my friends when they all learnt that I was unable to ride. I listened to the imagined contemptuous giggles and remarks of my Father's hideous coven of sisters.

My shallow courage and outrageous self-bicycling boasting had me turning once again to prayer. Insofar as God had divinely answered my initial prayer and, I was sure, had a hand in procuring my bicycle, he would have gifted me the ability to sit astride the machine and pedal forth confidently.

I finally trembled into sleep, having been told so many times that tomorrow never comes. But sadly, I knew this one would.

Comes the High Tide

Comes the high tide fire-frosted to the shoreline
Covering the ancient stones with sting and tingle
Sheets pulled tight, canvas flapping thunder
Stars alight in the twinkling of her eye
She cuts the water with her prow
Swinging the boom into a feathering dawn
Sailing on crests into the risen edge of day

A chilling kiss burns splashing rock to cover
A chilling kiss before the first birdsong
Still comes the lapping tide ever forward
Running to the jangle tangle of the wetlands
As the Medina spirits up its curling mists
Before dark and mystic waters
Before the Solent's edge has all light to see

Silently the tidal river, creek and marshland
Medina rises within reed banks of dream

The Lesson

The cold morning air was hanging on the trees as the sun splintered prisms of jewelled lights into the frosty air. A dancing cloud of mist rolled over the icy river Medina as the old floating bridge rattled towards me. The metallic grinding ring of chains and bridge gates opening heralded me and my Hercules Artisan's crossing from West Cowes to East Cowes.

Today was Monday, Boxing Day, and everyone I met was excited and in high spirits, wishing one and all a *Happy Christmas* and a *Happy New Year* as it was fast approaching. Earlier, I had walked my new shiny bicycle up and down Moorgreen Road to the cricket field several times, due to the fact I was unable to ride it, but in the hope I might solicit admiring glances from passers-by. None had been forthcoming.

It was nearly half eleven when I reached 9 Adelaide Grove, the home of my Father. Opening the tall wooden gate that led into a small backyard, I stood my bicycle up against a blackened coal bunker and entered the house through the ever-open back door. Passing the small scullery, I stood looking around the little sitting room. It was bedecked with Christmas cards and dressed for the yuletide in faded paper chains that had seen better days, whilst a sad drooping Christmas tree flickered a welcome with its meagre string of lights. The sad ensemble smiled back at me in comfortable disarray. The heavy air of yesterday's Christmas lunch was imbued into every nook and cranny. A meagre coal fire flickered in the hearth, fighting to heat the small room, its dancing light brightening the tired tinsel decoration which was wrapped around the brass coal scuttle.

The quiet serenity was suddenly broken by voices and loud barking from the scullery as my Grandmother Hilda and Tic, arguing the merits of winter gardening, burst into the room with the ever-yapping Sandy dancing excitedly around their feet.

Grandmother Hilda smiled broadly and her bright blue eyes twinkled when she spotted me sitting on the small brass fender beside the fireplace.

'Well, bugger me, look what the cat's brought in,' she said, clapping her hands in delight. 'It's our Stan's nipper. You won't find your Dad here, he's gone down the Vic early with your Uncle Roy. There's a bit of do on today.'

Midst the chaos of the moment I bumble-mumbled seasonal greetings, proffering a small gift for Tic which I knew to be cigarettes and a gift box of talc and fancy soap for Grandmother Hilda.

Tic nodded back his appreciation for the gift and, pushing back his cap, pointed to the window.

'Is that your new bike your Dad got you for Christmas outside nipper, leaning on the coal bunker in the rain?' he growled loudly. 'If you want to see him you know where he is now. You'll probably catch him up on your new bike, if you're quick.'

I nodded in agreement and left, thankful at leaving the discomforting atmosphere. Looking back, I thought I saw the front room curtains twitch just for a second as I pushed my bicycle in the pouring rain down Falcon Road towards Clarence Road and the Victoria Tavern.

It had stopped raining when I reached the Vic at one o'clock and, leaning my bike up against the wall, I looked down the passage of the main entrance into the tavern. Soon after, Mrs Myram the landlady came out to ask me who I wanted. I explained to her who I was and she seemed to recall me – and, of course, there was no doubting she knew my Father. She returned shortly with a message from him saying he would not be too long, he was just finishing a quick game of darts, and in the meantime a bottle of lemonade and a bag of crisps would need to suffice. Mrs Myram smiled at me sweetly and asked if I'd had a lovely Christmas with lots of toys and then she gave me a mince pie. I told her, pointing to my bicycle leaning on the pub wall, that Dad had bought me it for Christmas but sadly I was unable to ride it and that I really needed him to teach me.

'Well dear, when he finishes his game of darts I shall go and have a word with him,' she said, turning back through the door and into the pub. She soon returned bringing me another mince pie. 'He'll be out to see you very soon dear, I'm sure.'

In one respect Mrs Myram was correct. My Father did come out of the pub, albeit well over an hour or so later, to find me sitting on an upturned beer crate with my coat pulled tight under my chin and my teeth chattering. My first and lasting impression of him as he barrelled noisily through the doorway, spilling out onto the pavement, was that of his round, red, grinning countenance and him wearing a red garish jumper banded by white dancing snowmen.

The next minute I was hoisted high into the air and swung around until I was giddy, as my Father lathered wet embraces that smelt of beer and tobacco upon me whilst wishing me the merriest of Christmas wishes. Finally, gasping for breath, he put me down. Panting and sweating profusely, he leaned against the tavern wall with both hands to regain his breath as I excitedly explained to him my dilemma with my bike.

'You mean you want me… to teach you… to ride the bugger,' he said, at which point he lost his balance, resulting in him dancing little sideways steps into the road. Stopping suddenly, he looked about him in a surprised manner and burst out laughing.

His movements were still unsteady when he approached the bicycle, took hold of the saddle and the handlebars, and lifted it off the ground.

'It's a big heavy bugger nipper,' he said, replacing the bike onto the ground and patting the saddle as you might a horse.

He began tucking his trouser bottoms into his socks.

'Been a while, but they say once you learn to ride you never forget.'

At that, he took hold of the handlebars, steering it out onto the road. Hurrying alongside, he attempted to foot the nearside pedal and swing his right leg over the crossbar. The sight of my Father blurred into a cacophony of expletives and metallic clatter, showering gravel, man and bicycle.

Unbeknownst to either of us, his brother Roy and some other men had been stood watching as events unfolded from the tavern's open door. Laughing, they helped lift my still cursing Father out of the tangle of bike. Still laughing, they helped my bleeding and limping Father back into the pub.

'Could have killed himself, stupid old sod!' said Uncle Roy, shaking his head and stooping to help pick up my bike. 'Silly old bugger. Your Dad has made a real mess of your new bike nipper, it's scratched to buggery and he's bent and scratched the mudguards. Just look at those handlebars. He's bent the buggers and broken the shopping basket. You'll need to twist those handlebars straight before you try and ride it again.'

My Father appeared again at the doorway together with Mrs Myram. He was sporting a bandaged hand and a nasty looking red gash across his nose. Walking towards me, it was noticeably clear that my Father was still somewhat unsteady, made worse by his hoppity limp. Mrs Myram was holding his arm.

'Well, Stan,' she said, 'I don't think you'll be doing that again in a hurry.'

My poor Father cut a very dishevelled and sad figure as he stood shaking his head and apologising, looking over at me and my twisted bike.

'Better if you on your way now nipper,' he said. 'It'll be dark before you get up home and we'll be sure to get an hour or so sometime next week, if I can manage it.'

Then he stopped and put his finger into the air.

'Oh bugger!' he exclaimed as an afterthought. 'I almost forgot nipper, it's New Year next week and I expect we are all going to be busy. Better leave it for a week or two.'

Fighting back the tears, I agreed and turned around, beginning the long push back to Moorgreen Road in West Cowes. The light was dying and Clarence Road looked cold and grey in the drizzling fret that was drifting in from the Solent. I turned, still waving as I watched the last of the small group of men go back through the tavern doors into the jolly yuletide warmth of the tap room.

The desolation and complete despair that I felt at that moment, as I pushed my broken Hercules Artisan bicycle into the dying light, was amplified a thousand times over when the bright lights of Mr French's Bicycle Shop came into view. Displaying in the centre of his window was a brand-new Jack Taylor drop-handlebar sports bike in bright azure blue and a saddle as narrow as a pencil.

Standing there dreaming into Mr French's shop, I became aware that the pathetic image of myself was being reflected straight back at me. Stood shivering in the rain with my broken bike, my self-pity immediately turned into furious rage.

The rage was not aimed at my Father and his drunken, tedious antics. It was aimed at me. Only me. That was far more deserved. It was entirely my fault that I could not ride a bicycle. How long had I pretended? I had lied and lied and lied and at that moment in that cold grey light, I made myself a promise. I vowed that I would somehow fix and ride that damn bike proficiently before I would ever contact my Father again.

Boys on Bikes

Only I can see the where and who
The why of me into the furthest distance
As I pedal my bicycle down York Avenue
I see the rain crossing the faraway Solent
Watch white handkerchiefs sail into the wind

Grey Mr Godsland, spectacles upon his nose
Welcoming dawn through his open door
The tight bundle binding cuts into his fingers
As he sits sorting papers in Castle Street
Filling bags of yesterday's news for boys on bikes

The stinging wind and rain is free
Cutting my face with cold dark winter
Wrought iron gates and raggity path
Man's best friend throws tail and teeth
Growling at the morning news upon the mat

Saturday morning's grey ache grind
The heavy *County Press* smells of ink
Thumbs up for Pompey's sailor boy
His winning ways taking my breath away
As I pedal past the Vics on Beatrice Avenue

The King's Cinema

Pushing through side exits, spilling out onto the street, the bustling rush of children leaving the cinema would all go blinking into the bright midday liken to noisy moles emerging from the darkness.

Many a shootout and sword fight had been won and lost. We had even fought hand to hand battles with Nazi stormtroopers or a band of Apache braves. All was played out with noise and gusto upon the battlefields of Church Path and Well Road as we made our way home from King's Cinema in East Cowes.

Almost all our initial cinema going was borne out of the Saturday Morning Matinees; there were always a couple of short feature films and a mixture of crazy cartoons. These morning matinees were always extremely noisy and boisterous occasions, and the feature film was always the catalyst for whatever battle or challenge awaited the homeward journey.

As I grew older, I began spending less time in East Cowes (possibly due to the fraught and unhappy home life that I was experiencing), choosing instead to visit my Grandmother or my Auntie Norma. Very often I would visit the Royalty Cinema in Cowes, sitting happily in the ninepennies and soon lost in fantasy or thrills, enjoying my tub of Walls ice cream at the interval. Sometimes I would be joined by my cousin Judith or my lovely old Aunt Min.

There was no doubt though that the King's in East Cowes was by far my favourite cinema of all upon the whole island. Although it was hardly a fair comparison insofar as I had only visited one other outside of Cowes, that being the Medina Cinema in Newport. On that occasion I had queued in the rain with my Grandmother, who had promised to take me to see *Davy Crocket: King of the Wild Frontier*. Oh, how desperately I wanted to be the first boy in East Cowes to be seen wearing a fur raccoon hat with a dangle-down tail like Davy Crocket wore and to own a sheath knife with a Jim Bowie curve. I sang the catchy theme song from the film long and hard until my throat rasped, but sad to say I never did realise my dreams. No hat. No knife.

I have had an unexplainable lifelong love for the ambiance and blissful warmth of Italian restaurants from the very first time I watched the now famous 'Spaghetti Scene' in *The Lady and the Tramp*. I truly fell in love with this soulful and touching animation and am still happy to watch it to this day.

My love for this cherished film is amplified by a certain other memory. I had been taken to see the film by my Auntie Norma when it came out in 1955. She had come over to East Cowes when she finished her work at the Co-op offices on York Street and after spending twenty minutes or so in the queue, we were in. Without exception, Auntie Norma chose to sit in the more expensive seats towards the back of the cinema. The lights were up and the sweet strains of Mantovani were playing as people streamed through to take their seats. The whole auditorium was buzzing with excitement; I had been told that the film had even been mentioned on the radio. I could not recall ever seeing the King's Cinema being as full. There was no doubting the fact it was going to be a full house.

Amidst the general hubbub in the cinema, I heard a piercing voice rising above all others ringing out one instruction after another.

'Please do excuse me. Maria, further, further.'

I recognised it. I remembered it well from the Spurs Café and this irritating and insistent voice was closing towards us.

'No, Maria darling, go further down, look, are you blind darling, there are two seats together in the middle, go on, push on.'

The two vacant seats to my immediate right noisily folded forward... Maria Jones was sitting next to me! My heartbeat was audible. I could not believe it was happening. Things like this were not possible.

Our eyes met for the longest second the world or universe has ever recorded. She smiled into mine and I smiled back, lost in seas of brightness and wonder.

Bending forward, she whispered a husky 'hello' and with my eyes glazed I replied with a soundless nod.

At the zenith of the 'Spaghetti Scene' she reached over and squeezed my hand for just that moment. It was as if an explosion of white fire had seared through my being. I swore to myself that I would never wash that embrace of connection away.

'Do you know that young lady?' asked my Auntie Norma, leaning down to me.

I was embarrassed and shrugged a not too convincing 'no' as the rising heat burst over my cheeks like a rash. Fortunately, we were in the darkness of the cinema.

When the film was over the house lights gradually came up, the National Anthem playing loud and long from huge black speakers on either side of the screen. Auntie Norma tugged at my arm to ensure my cooperation as we joined the greater part of the audience, standing obediently in silent respect. As the last strains faded, I was eager to say a quiet goodbye to Maria. But when I looked, I was amazed to discover that both Maria and her Mother had left quietly whilst the National Anthem had been playing.

I glimpsed them both in the melee beside the main door as people began bustling forward. For one brief moment I saw Maria clearly silhouetted in the exit. My hand came up to wave, but she was gone.

Although we never did have our own 'Spaghetti Scene', I have never forgotten those blossoming moments of first love, the brief touch of her hand upon mine, or her lovely face.

Regretfully, I never saw Maria again.

Memories of Maria

How warm the morning bright is breaking
My love
Smile sweet summer chases freckle shadows beneath her hat
Red silk scarf wind whipping
Moments of her perfume in the air
Her words carry on the wind drowning far out to sea
Softly heard within shells upon some distant shore
My love
Green her sun-sparkle eyes flash like splashes from the sea
Taking my hand into hers she smiles
We laugh and kiss like children
The taste of sea and perfume
August looms across the blue sky following the horizon
My love

Cousin Ray and the American

Late summer's lazy afternoons rolled easily into evening. Lines of deepening lavender blushed the distant mainland as Fawley's roman candle flare stack began to brighten the sky. Children's swings hung desolate, still as soldiers on their long brown iron chains. Dried flakes of green paint curled on a small wooden roundabout which sat sad and motionless.

The Jubilee Recreation Ground in East Cowes, or as it is better known by locals, The Rec, was the wide-open green space gifted to the town by Lord Gort and bordered by the beautifully mature trees that edge both sides of York Avenue. The top of The Rec was for the sole use of young children; there was a small area for swings, a slide, a small wooden roundabout, and my favourite: the gondola-motion American swing.

'I bet you haven't heard the latest Everly Brothers record,' drawled my cousin Ray, leaning motionless on the swing poles over one end of the American. 'It's called 'Dream'.'

Ray was a year or so older than me, his island accent slow and rich – and everything I wanted to be: self-assured, casually confident and always (or so it seemed) able to demonstrate a wider breadth of knowledge on things than myself or my immediate peer group. Although always casual, his fashion sense was just that little more stylish: he wore a necklace, turned his cuffs back, and instead of plain black plimsoles he would wear American baseball boots. And as though that wasn't enough, he was good looking, with his long dark hair combed in an Elvis Presley style.

I feigned a quizzical expression, moreover to give Ray the impression that I was au fait with the latest in pop music, and then replied as casually as I could muster, 'No, I don't think so, is it their latest release?'

'Yeah nipper. The Everlys, they're bloody fantastic, yeah,

they're something special.'

Ray was shading his eyes against the low sun as he looked from his standing position on the American, down across The Rec to the beautiful building that was the Frank James Hospital with its iconic verdigris clock tower. Turning back to face me, he asked: 'What do you think about 'My Baby Loves the Western Movies'?'

Never heard of it would have been the honest answer. Instead, I said, 'That's a Buddy Holly song, isn't it?'

'That'll be the day,' said Ray quietly.

It was a beautiful warm summer's evening. What followed, as we both sat gently swinging into the blue of twilight, was the vilification of pop singers and their bands and a breakdown of recent and current releases which Ray and his older sister, Anita, had purchased at Radio Resco to play on her HMV record player.

It was getting late. Out over Calshot Spit and the distant Southampton Water, smoke-grey clouds floated slowly across the dimming line of a burnt orange glow just below the horizon. Heavenly shades of night were falling.

Resco's

It was one of those bright crisp Cowes mornings; the wind was cutting and getting up, swirling about the Medina's estuary. The river swans were enjoying bread thrown to them by a rather plump lady in a bright green coat, whilst her tall thin husband lingered behind within a cloud of blue smoke as he attempted to light a cigarette in the chilling gusts. The large overhanging clock at the ticket office clunked loudly as the hour changed. It was now ten o'clock. I stamped my feet to keep warm as the noise of the clanking, grinding, floating bridge grew ever closer. Moments later, crunching to a standstill, it had reached the sloping slipway.

I was on my way back to East Cowes. For the past week or so I had been staying with my Auntie Norma in Gurnard.

The half a crown and the cigarette packet containing two Players Weights which she had handed me before I'd left were still in my pocket, together with a packet of Garibaldi biscuits, a gift for my Mother and my change of clothes packed neatly away in my brown paper carrier bag. Passing the 'Umbrella Tree' at the bottom of York Avenue, I noticed a small gathering across the road at the wide entrance frontage of Radio Resco. Television had been with us for many years, but in early 1955 television sets were still a rare sight indeed and here at the bottom of York Avenue, Resco's had taken delivery of as many as ten.

Radio Resco was owned by Mr Harold Bowen and he had set up a television outside on his forecourt. A small crowd gazed on in wonderment as an array of fizzled, snowy, jagged lines danced across an exceedingly small screen on a television the size of a sideboard.

'Our John got one for the Coronation a couple of years ago, do you remember?' said the lady who had been feeding the swans earlier. 'They watched it up home with the family. Our Vera went up to see it, don't you remember?'

'Lucky they could afford it,' said her husband, squinting at the silver blizzard on the screen. 'Your Vera said it was a bit blurred.'

Two men were unwinding cable from the shop to the television set.

'Now wait until you see this, this is a new kind of aerial cable,' said Mr Bowen, his arms on his hips and pointing up to the roof of his shop. 'This is a much better one than was there before.'

A series of tall steel rods forming an 'H' shape was affixed to the side of Mr Bowen's chimney stack – to my mind, looking very much like the one that had been there for the last couple years. Mr Bowen was explaining to us that the television signal was now coming from a completely different source on the mainland and was far more powerful and therefore the reception would be significantly improved.

'Unfortunately, I am unable to demonstrate the new and improved picture quality due to the fact that the television programming 'start up' is not until one o'clock. And even then, it's only likely to be a test card.'

The small group of people that had gathered sighed collectively and moved on. All, that is, but the plump lady in the bright green coat and her chain-smoking husband.

'What's one of these,' he asked, pointing to a large television cabinet whilst coughing through a cloud of cigarette smoke, 'and one of those fancy radiograms going to cost me a week?'

Although Mr Bowen, in that moment of wisping nicotine, was partially hidden by smoke, it was as though someone had turned the brightest of spotlights upon him. His eyes opened wide in a joyous twinkle and his round brown face lit up like one of his silver dancing television screens. A gold tooth flashed in the bright cold sunshine. Sweeping his arm majestically, he gestured the couple graciously towards the open entrance of his shop, reminiscent of the spider ushering flies into his parlour.

Down Shore

Rocking, rolling
Riding upon salt-crested waves
Down shore
High upon a sea of green glass
Golden stones
Splashing emeralds
Between tip and toe
Down shore
Tangled liquid after music
Surging rhythm of the sea
Pulsing to the anywhere
Of the music where I need to be
Forever and all time
Leaving me swimming the long song
Down shore

Up and Running

I had always dreaded the time of year when the clocks were required to be turned back and darkness prevailed, winter awaiting us all with its icy bated breath.

Dark winter evenings were spent beside our small coal fire, listening to the BBC Light Programme on the radio – *The Goon Show*, *In Town Tonight* and my most favourite of all, *Journey into Space*. My Mother and I did not have a television set in our home. Instead, we listened to the radio and although by this time most of my friend's families were boasting the ownership of a television, we were unable to afford such a luxury. However, a recent member of this elite class of television viewers and an avid fan to boot, so it seems, was my very own Grandmother Beatrice in West Cowes. My Uncle Donald and Aunt Min had recently arranged for a television set on HP to ensure she was kept abreast of current affairs, entertainment and company whilst they were at the pub. Initially, she spurned the very idea of such a thing, but very quickly became its most ardent supporter. So much so, that for Christmas she decided to arrange to hire another set for my Mother and me.

We had both been spending some time at my Grandmother's in West Cowes and lately Mother was making great progress regaining her health. Evening discussions had centred around the fast-approaching Christmas holidays and I was amazed and thrilled to learn that my Grandmother had decided to spend Christmas with us at Kent House. She also announced the great news regarding the gift of a television and that she had arranged with Harold Bowen to ensure that the correct aerial was erected and fitted. Our brand-new television would be up and running perfectly prior to Christmas. Harold himself had promised my Grandmother that he would have everything in place and all that was necessary and in readiness for a perfect picture for no later than Christmas Eve.

This was like a dream coming true and I was giddy with excitement. I was hardly able to contain my longing for the Christmas holidays to start; this was going to be a Christmas like no other…

Christmas Day, 1957

Bright overhead decorations in the busy narrow streets of Cowes and all the shop windows were bedecked for yuletide. From every doorway the smells and sounds of Christmas were all about us. Adorned Christmas trees twinkled in bow windows, holly wreaths hung from front doors and there was even a hint of snow in the air. People were jolly and wishing each other good cheer and I could not help myself – I just had to stop at Radio Resco to watch the televisions inanely flickering their silver light in his window display.

At long last it was Christmas Eve. I had travelled over West to meet my Grandmother and accompany her to Kent House. In all the years that I had lived there, and apart from my Father on the odd occasion, we had never ever had a visitor stay overnight.

Grandmother's bags were laden with mince pies, cakes, presents and other goodies. Her bags were very heavy, but I didn't mind as we struggled up York Avenue to the entrance of Kent House. We were met at the large front entrance by my Mother, who looked so happy. She was in smart slacks and looked attractive with her hair brushed back and wearing lipstick. After throwing her arms around my Grandmother she led her up the winding stone stairway to our small flat. I followed, carrying Grandmother's heavy holdall and brown paper carrier bag. My Grandmother was ushered into the small hallway, but I stood back, lingering on the doormat, not quite knowing whether or not I would be allowed to enter. I was always wary of my Mother's Voices, but she grabbed my hand and pulled me through. I was quickly out of my shoes and into damp, cold slippers and given instructions to take Grandmother's bags through to the bedroom which she was to share with my Mother.

The bedroom was warm and welcoming, a cheery coal fire blazed from behind a brass guard in the small fireplace.

'Mr Bowen from Resco's is due in an hour,' shouted my Mother from the scullery. 'That just leaves us time to have a cup of tea. I'm going to have a word with that Harold Bowen when he arrives. Just look at that wire pinned to the wall into that strange plug thing on the skirting board. Oh, I don't know, it's not as though I don't have enough to do. The aerial man was here this morning for hours fiddling about on the roof and he said Harold would be here about three o'clock.'

My Mother had been, of course, referring to the aerial cable and television socket which was now waiting in readiness for Mr Bowen and the television. My excitement was overwhelming and I could hardly contain myself with the sheer giddy joy of soon being able to sit and watch our own television.

Half an hour or so later there was a knock on the door. When my Mother opened it, Mr Bowen and his aerial man were outside unpacking the television set from its cardboard wrappings. Much to my Grandmother's consternation my Mother immediately set to placing walk-through towels from the front door to the lounge.

Grandmother made up for the less than warm welcome, enthusing and embracing Harold like a long-lost love.

Fifteen minutes or so later, the television and a smart walnut veneer two-door cabinet which closed over when it was not in use had been installed. The fourteen-inch screen was dazzling us with its snowy wonder. I was so happy.

Before the men left, my Mother had warmed a plate of mince pies and brought through another pot of tea and placed them on a card table whilst we all watched *I Love Lucy*. I was so excited that I clenched my fists together and punched the air in sheer joy. Alas, I misjudged my wild flying fists of exultation and punched myself hard under my nose. For a second or two I was numb and confused and fell back onto the floor where I had been kneeling. I soon became aware of voices. Harold was sitting me up whilst my Mother was chastising me for being stupid and showing off. As I opened my mouth to explain, I felt the first warm, sticky trickle dripping off my chin.

'Oh my God, he's bleeding!' shrieked my Mother. 'Take him out in the scullery!' she shrilled. 'Quick, get a wet cloth from under the sink to wipe his blood off the lino!' she shouted. 'Oh no, it's on the rug!' she sobbed.

My Grandmother had led me to the kitchen and was endeavouring to staunch the heavy flow from my nose by leaning my head backwards and holding the wet, cold, bucket cloth under my nose. All this served to choke me as the flow of blood was coursing down my throat. As I moved forward, sticky crimson clots of blood were plopping onto the scullery floor.

'This is a really serious nosebleed,' said Harold. 'I know people that have died of these types of bleeds if they can't be stopped.'

Although I was bleeding profusely, I was all too aware of what Mr Bowen was saying and really was wishing that he had not.

Mr Bowen promptly returned to his shop to lock up for the Christmas holidays, but on his way down York Avenue summoned Doctor Downs as a matter of urgency.

When the doctor arrived my Grandmother took charge, immediately explaining the situation and quickly removing the heaps of bloodied towelling. She also supplied the good doctor with a hot mince pie and a large measure of whisky from the bottle my Mother had been given for Christmas.

My poor Mother was looking haggard and worried again, spending most of her time at the scullery sink wringing out bloodied towels.

'Yes, yes, yes,' droned Doctor Downs to Grandmother Beatrice. 'I am well acquainted with this young man's ability to display posterior epistaxis by the bucketful.'

Grandmother Beatrice smiled weakly. Nodding, she proffered another mince pie and refill for his whisky. Declining, he bent over me, examining my nose with a pencil torch and then carefully inserting thin rubber plugs up into the furthest reaches of my nasal passages. This had the effect of staunching the ongoing and outward flow of blood, but I was still swallowing a good deal and feeling very sick.

'The bleeding will soon slow and stop in about ten minutes or so,' he said. 'Just be a good lad and sit quietly.'

When he had completed his very messy task the doctor took my Mother and Grandmother to one side and said in a low voice, 'This young man must be kept quiet and very still for at least three days, nothing exciting or physical. Best place for him is sitting up reading a good book in bed. Do not on any account let him laugh or shout out loud, sing or the like. And whilst I fully appreciate that you have a television set, please keep him from watching as staring at a bright screen is the last thing the boy needs.'

Looking at the bloodied look of despair upon my face, he pointed to our new television.

'Sorry m'lad, I know full well it's Christmas, but I'm afraid it's a definite no no. I told both your Mother and your Grandmother you would be better reading a good book and benefit by staying away from any bright lights or excitement.'

He wished us all a very *Merry Christmas* and a *Prosperous New Year* and further informed us that he would be returning before the New Year to check all was well. With that, he bade the ladies goodnight and left.

Both my Mother and Grandmother did their best to make my small bedroom cheery by bringing tinsel to hang over the foot of the bed and some Christmas cards on my bookshelf. My face was frozen by the inner healing process and the intrusion of the rubber bungs deep within my nostrils, and for the same reason talking and eating was almost impossible.

'It's a great pity, I know,' said my Grandmother. 'There will be plenty of time over the New Year to enjoy the television. Let's get you well first.'

The medication administered by the doctor was influencing me and I began to feel very sleepy. Although propped up in a sitting position with pillows all about me and being aware of my instructions not to bleed would not make sleeping easy.

My Mother and Grandmother bent over me, kissing me gently on my forehead. Before leaving, Grandmother said, 'Remember, it's Christmas Day in the morning,' and pausing, she winked and added: 'Presents.'

My Mother was looking at both of us. Drawn and close to tears, she nodded.

'God bless, sleep tight,' they both called from the small hall.

I was desolate and heartbroken. This was supposed to have been a Christmas to remember. A special Christmas. A proper Christmas.

Frosty, early silver light was breaking and cast dancing shadows over my bedroom ceiling. I was becoming aware of my still propped position and predicament. I was also aware that my bedroom was icy cold as I reached out and put on my bedside light. A moment or two later the bedroom door opened and both my Mother and Grandmother bounded through, heaping careful, quieted kisses upon me and at the same time wishing me a *Merry Christmas*. Breakfast of sorts was served, but unable to eat I sucked lukewarm tea through a straw. A little later as gifts were being brought through to my bed, I was still completely unable to respond to them. I could neither smile nor talk properly and as we exchanged gifts I was only able to respond by gestures and grunts.

Two of my gifts were particularly special insomuch as my Mother had given me a pair of beautiful suede sheepskin gloves, whilst my Grandmother had knitted a balaclava and matching scarf for me. But she had also given me a book entitled *Two Years Before the Mast* by Richard Henry Dana Jr.

The aroma of Christmas lunch is like no other and was gently wafting through to me from the small oven in the scullery. It rose upon ever-increasing waves of delicious temptation. Whilst my nose ached, my tastebuds panged and dribbled and soon lunch was served…

…I was spoon-fed liquidised Christmas lunch with gravy followed by smashed Christmas pudding and custard. I was so hungry it really did not matter any longer. All my worst memories and childhood nightmares of Mother's illness and the Voices came flooding back; Christmas Day could not get any worse. Then I was given some of my prescribed medication and told to rest.

Soon, the clattering metallic sounds of washing and clearing up, laughter and jolly conversation was drifting through.

'We are going to watch *The Queen's Speech* at three o'clock,' shouted Mother from the lounge. 'We'll be through to see you as soon as she has finished.'

I reached out, slipping on my new suede gloves, balaclava and scarf. No doubt I must have looked very strange sat up in my bed dressed like Captain Scott of the Antarctic. I stretched to pick up my new book, which was not easy to do in sheepskin gloves. Suddenly, the book flew up into the air and although I tried to catch it mid-flight the corner of the hardback and its full weight hit me hard across my nose. At first, there was nothing more than the recall of the sharp impact. I held my breath. The book had landed open upon my lap. I noticed a picture of a brig in full sail and began reading when suddenly the bright white sails in front of me splashed red with blood, followed by more splashes, quicker and quicker, splashes on my bed, down the woollen chin of my balaclava, drip, drop, dripping with heavy plops upon my lovely suede gloves. The ruby red splashes were relentless.

There have been many Christmas Days and lunches since then, but there have been few quite as memorable and none as painful.

Posterior Epistaxis Maximus

Malena breath
A stomach full of blood
Deep dark
Comes the smell of chrysanthemum
Metallic iron flaking edge
Rusting old chains
Oh! precious flow of life
How you were wasting
Tasting of salt tears
Fears that tomorrow will be poorly dressed

Loneliness helps concentrate the mind
Dulls the aching tickle
Hot crimson trickle drip dropping
Stopping to splash its signature
Hideous confusion swallowed down
Beginning to drown
In my own life's blood

The Cannon

In addition to selling the town televisions and radios and all other manner of electrical goods, from after the last day of Cowes Week until well after the smoke of Guy Fawkes' bonfire night had cleared, Harold Bowen of Radio Resco also sold fireworks.

No more than any other boys of our age, we enjoyed the excitement of setting off fireworks illicitly and I particularly enjoyed the making of mischief. For example, the experimental effects of bangers and squibs in cowpats, or firing rockets and marine flares which hung in the night sky before slowly spiralling earthward to crash in a myriad of splashing orange sparks upon the ground.

It was that time of year again; the summer of 1955 was now consigned to memory and autumn frost and short, stunted days drew night in stark and damp. I recall it was on such a dank evening that my friend Sherf showed me a small cannon that he had fashioned from a spent .303 brass rifle shell case.

He had mounted it by wiring and tying the shell case onto a small block of wood, allowing the end of this mini-cannon to project by an inch or two. He had then drilled a small hole through the top towards the closed end of the shell case and set about filling the cannon with *just enough* gunpowder (removed from a banger firework), pushing cotton wool and finally a ball bearing into the breach end with the help of small gimlet. He had pushed a split matchstick into the hole at the rear of the cannon to act as a fuse (ensuring its red tip was in view), before positioning house bricks on each side in the event of recoil. He then set up a tin can full of water ten feet away and level with the cannon to serve as the target.

Carefully lighting the exposed match head with a long straw

taper, he stepped back. A moment later, after the fizz of the igniting match head, there was small bang and a long flash of flame issued from the little cannon. The tin can flew into the air, spraying water in all directions. On inspection, it was found to be punctured very nearly in two by the impact of the small ball bearing.

Although we had purchased and examined very nearly all of Mr Bowen's firework selection, we had discovered that the maximum gunpowder that could be obtained from an individual firework was from a Payne's Squib. Thereafter, the gradual development from the .303 shell knew no bounds. Our little mine of pyrotechnics had soon dried up and we were now purchasing 410 shotgun cartridges and using them as the accelerant agent, which did save a lot of time; there was no more carefully gutting squibs and bangers to extract their precious black powder.

There had been a few little mishaps on the way whilst we experimented with and developed our homemade cannons. As our confidence grew (although it is probably more honest to say Sherf's confidence), so too did the size of our cannons. I recall one such cannon measuring approximately eighteen inches in length, fashioned from mild steel conduit piping with a diameter of approximately four or so centimetres, the breach end hammered flat, again mounted on a large block of heavy wood. We set about testing it down in the woods close to the Bommy Building, shattering chucks of old brickwork with old glass alley marbles as missiles.

Sherf had another idea and suggested that if the missile we used was heavier more streamlined, ideally bullet shaped, it could fly further. This resulted in us digging a small hole in the ground and filling it with builders' sand, pushing our fingers straight down into it as far as we could reach and thus forming a mould. We gave up our lead toy soldiers and used any other scrap lead we could find, melting it in an old brass jam pan that we had purloined from Mike Brinton's Mother's kitchen. Once the lead was sufficiently liquified, we poured it carefully into the finger moulds and waited for it to cool. When the lead was extracted, it formed a weighty, almost bullet shaped projectile. Cleaned, rubbed and buffed, it would serve as an ideal missile.

After a number of tests over the fields – always ensuring first that neither Prince nor cattle were grazing – we aimed our cannon at certain trees whereupon we had placed a white painted dustbin lid as a target. Even at a distance of a hundred yards we quickly realised that our cannon was well able to fire much further than we had at first estimated.

East Cowes Castle

Formerly a grand estate and home, East Cowes Castle was by now no more than a faded beauty, a dilapidated ruin. It had been the country seat of John Nash, one of the foremost architects of the Regency and Georgian eras, who was responsible for designing Buckingham Palace, Clarence House and, of course, his home here on the island. By the mid-1950s, it was completely ruined and deserted, with the surrounding acreage of the once splendidly laid out grounds being cultivated into a fruit farm. Nonetheless, the building still presented an imposing sight across the fields, looking out and over the Solent.

'I reckon,' said Sherf, 'we could hit it from here.' He paused and cupped his hand over his eyes as he scanned the distance. 'Yeah, I think we could.'

'As the crow flies, the main tower can only be about half a mile or so, probably a bit less,' said Mike Brinton, as he squinted to focus more clearly.

In a general discussion that followed, the distance varied from a few hundred yards to over a mile. Whilst none of us thought that the cannon could not reach, we all agreed that there could be no definitive way of telling if we had hit the target or missed it.

'Tell you what,' announced Sherf, 'what about if Gus and Mike go over to the castle and go up to the top of the tower and wave a flag and we'll fire the cannon at you when we see it.'

An explosion of spluttering expletives followed from both me and Mike as we protested.

'If we don't fall off and break our bloody necks!' I opined. 'That old tower's falling to bits, it's really bloody dangerous.'

'Not only that!' shouted Mike, pointing a shaking finger at the cannon.

'Yeah, Mike's right,' I eagerly agreed. 'What about that bloody thing? It could kill us!'

'Nah! You daft buggers. Once you're up there and wave the flag and we see you, me and Phil will wave our flag back.'

'Then after we wave our flag,' said Phil, 'we'll count to five and I'll light the fuse.'

Philip Hunt was a bright, cheerful boy, who lived close by on Princess Close... but had always struck me as somewhat devious.

'So, have you two got that?' said Sherf. 'We will wave back at you and then after a count of five you duck down behind the battlements and we will fire the cannon.'

'Once you've both ducked down,' whispered Phil, smiling mischievously and laughing, 'you had better count to five again. Just in case.'

After another couple of run-throughs of the plan, we all decided that the next day was going to be the most suitable for our assault on East Cowes Castle Tower – it was forecast to be clear and most importantly, dry. We spent the rest of the day making the two flags, which were going to be essential for signalling, by tying old white pillowslips borrowed from Phil's Mother's laundry basket to thick bamboo canes.

Late autumn colours had faded to fawn through to tangerine as a cold stinging wind chased me and Mike as we set off together. We crossed the road that led to the Bommy Building, then quickly through the woods until we reached the old iron fence. We took turns carrying our white flag across Warner's fields, not that it was particularly heavy – we just liked the feel of carrying a fluttering flag. We stopped and looked back at the old tennis court field where Sherf and Philip were setting the cannon upon a gantry of bricks and blocks of wood. We were pleased we had chosen Sunday as our day to climb the tower and, careful to check that there was no one about that might attempt to chase us off the property, we ploughed on. Finally, we had reached the remnants of last summer's raspberry and blackberry gardens, now just a tangle of bush and bramble.

Most of the entrances and conservatory windows to this once grand building were boarded up. With extraordinarily little persuasion, the flimsy barricade of plywood and boarding soon yielded and we were both through. A minute or two later, we were standing at the small entrance beneath the spiralling stone steps leading to the top of tower. Climbing up the tower was no easy task, much of the outer winding stone stairway was loose and very suspect, and in places we had to help each other hand over hand to safety as some of the stone steps were no longer in existence. When at last we had reached the top of the tower, we entered through a small gothic arch onto a grey roundel stone roof, much of which was cracked and grown through with tufts of moss and weed.

Sherf and Phil had by now recalculated and decided to mount the cannon on a higher a platform, from where they agreed both the aim and trajectory would be better served. They laid their white flag down beside them as they busied themselves building the cannon battery. Every now and then they would take turns and scan the castle's ramparts, looking for any signs of a fluttering white flag.

The cannon was soon in readiness, mounted and powdered up and loaded with our homemade moulded lead projectile. The breach end would be made ready with a pinch of gunpowder when it was finally decided to light and fire.

'Any signs of the buggers yet?' enquired Sherf. 'They should have been there by now. I hope they haven't fallen off and broken their bloody necks in this wind.'

Both boys looked at each other and moments later burst into laughter. Then Phil let out a whoop of joy – he did not need a second look; he had seen a definite flash of white fluttering high on the largest of the castle towers.

'There they are!'

Both boys scanned into the far distance. Sherf cupped his hands to his mouth so that he might be heard, shouting out above the wind: 'Wave our flag Phil, let them know we have seen them.'

'Do you think they've seen us?' shouted Phil, struggling to keep hold of the madly fluttering flag.

There was suddenly a ripping sound, a momentary flash of white and the flag spiralled into the air. The wind carried it high, as flapping into a metal grey sky and looking like a broken seagull it soared, until it was out of sight.

After we had crawled on our bellies to the battlement parapets, Mike looked up and shouted, 'I think I can see them both.'

He was right, we could see them clearly beneath the trees standing next to what we assumed to be the cannon. The fields ran away from us like a green carpet and to our right we could see clear across the Solent to Fawley.

We could hear our pillow flag flapping and slapping above our heads. I was holding onto the stick for dear life as we both tried to peer between the battlements to the fields beyond, where the cannon should be set up and ready to fire.

'Can you see them? No sign of a bloody flag anywhere.'

Suddenly Mike yelled, 'Look! There they are! I can see them. There they are waving their arms... Where's their flag?'

'I've no bloody idea,' I hissed hoarsely. 'They're jumping about like mad waving at us. I think they must want us to wave our flag. Now remember Mike, east to west, east to west, heads down and count nice and slow one to five and *make sure you keep your bloody head down.*'

Mike stood up and exacted the white flag semaphore as instructed and then quickly dropped to his knees. He joined me as we huddled and crouched behind a stone battlement.

We both remained flattened to the cold grey stone when we

heard clearly the distant but distinct crack of the cannon. We clung like limpets to one another other for what seemed an eternity when we heard a loud whining then thud just below our battlement, no more than ten feet below us. There was no doubt whatsoever, something extremely hard had just hit the tower wall.

When we leaned over to examine the tower below there was evidence of damage to dressed stonework: a clean white scar of exposed stone.

Although we, the gang of four, all excitedly shared the moment of our joint success over and over, none of us were ever to fire a cannon of any sort again. Nor for that matter did any of us ever return to East Cowes Castle. Soon after that, no more than a couple of years, we had all for one reason or another drifted apart; boys into men, with wives and families, all of us travelling a different road.

Every firework night I vividly recall our adventures – especially when the smell of sulphur and gunpowder smoke fills the air. My mind goes back to those dangerous experiments that we undertook, but I still feel a sense of pride in our innovation and initiatives. Now, after all the years as I listen to children laugh and enjoy the thrill of bonfires and fireworks, bangers and rockets, I am more than happy just to take another slice of parkin and a nip of something Scottish... and smile to myself as I watch the younger ones, excited and wide-eyed, playing with their sparklers.

Ian Sherfield went on to become an extraordinarily successful and renowned Electrical Engineer, responsible for the management of the grid connection and electricity supply to the infrastructure to the UK side of the Channel Tunnel. He is also the author of a superb book entitled *Pictorial History of East Cowes Castle* and has also written a history of electricity on the Isle of Wight entitled *Electric Wight*.

The Seat of John Nash, Esq.

Can you see it?
There, it sits in the green fields
Upon the highest point
There it is, against the sky
Catching the light above the trees
Beyond lies the sea
Sea tied by a golden band of stones

Beyond lies the sea
With its salty chill upon the ever
Fade away green to a far blue edge
High grey stones climbing to silver
Towers and turrets watch over the small town
Elegant windows have closed their blind eyes
Doors lock in forever their last welcoming

Beside the flower gardens perfumed bloom
Beside the shadow of your southernmost tower
Sleeps forever in white chalk stones
Sleeps forever in sand and shells

Sleep in forever peace John and MaryAnn
Their hound sitting sejant beside them ever

All the flowers are dying John
Whisper thistle, whisper thorn
Came then winters
Came then storms
All of those yesterdays
All of those yesterdays are somewhere
Blowing in the wind

Northwood, 1954

On a fine day, from our tiny scullery window in Kent House, I could see clear across the sparkle of the Medina to the jagged, green, tree-lined edge of Northwood.

My Grandmother had planned to take me on the bus for a visit to her brother Harry and his lifelong friend Bert. Their house was on Wyatts Lane, not too far from the Horseshoe Inn on Newport Road at Northwood. They had fought in both wars and had always lived together in an old, rambling, yellow brick house fitted with faded, painted wooden shutters and a tangle of red vine almost obscuring the wide front entrance. At the rear was a large walled garden, edged in raised flower beds full of roses with cordoned fruit trees surrounding the whole garden. In the centre, in neat, raised beds, every vegetable imaginable grew in profusion. An arched doorway opened into an adjoining orchard where apple, pear, plum and greengage grew upon a verdant carpet of waving tall grasses and wildflowers. Butterflies flashed and darted from flower to flower whilst birdsong and the industrious drone of honeybees filled the air.

Grandmother Beatrice pushed open the side gate that led into the garden. Carrying her heavy basket of homemade treats, she called out Harry's name and was surprised to see Bert hurrying down the path towards us.

'Harry has gone over to Mad Masie's and old Aunt Carrie's place up Oxford Street,' said Bert, after an initial hug and kiss. 'Been a fire or some such. It's long since out, but he's gone up to see what he can do.' He stood for a moment, hands on hips and raising his eyes to the heavens. 'Silly old buggers the pair of them, burnt the shed down.'

'Their shed!' shrieked Grandmother.

'I was just about to go up myself,' said Bert, at which point he caught sight of the bulging basket, 'but as you are here and their fire's out, I'll not bother. Come on in Beatie and I'll make you both a cup of—'

'We will do no such thing Bert,' said Grandmother, cutting him short. 'We'll need to go and help Carrie and Masie as quickly as possible.' She turned on her heels, pushing both Bert and me in front of her, and shrilled: 'Come on boys and be quick about it!'

Wisps of curling blue smoke drifted lightly out onto the street, dancing down onto the drooping blood red peonies until caught in an eddying zephyr it rose over the trees, out to the river. Uncle Harry was in the front garden adding to an already large pile of acrid, smelling, charred timber as we arrived at Aunt Carrie's house.

'I won't kiss you Beatie, I'm covered in soot and muck, besides...' Harry's voice trailed off, as the front door opened directly behind him.

'Don't think he'll be finished for a little while yet Beatie,' said a voice creaked with age from within the dark interior of the open front porch door.

The shaky croak belonged to Aunt Carrie, who looked and sounded to me as though she was at the very least a hundred years old. She stood peering and blinking into the bright sunlight where we were all standing.

I had on occasion overheard my Grandmother and my Mother talk of Aunt Carrie and her spinster daughter Masie. I knew they lived together at Northwood, but other than that I had never seen or met them in my life. Carrie was always referred to as Carrie, but Masie referred to as 'Mad Masie'. I had never inquired as to why this should be, I merely accepted it as an eccentric family description (although I suspected that they were not blood relations, as usage of the term 'Auntie' was commonplace as a term of respect). My perception of what these ladies would look like from descriptions given by my Mother, Grandmother and Uncle Donald was so far removed from the reality.

Aunt Carrie was waving her arms, wildly beckoning us all to enter, being sure to remove our shoes and leave them in the porch. We all did as were bade, except for Uncle Harry who had elected to stay in the garden to complete his clearing of the still smouldering shed. We followed Aunt Carrie into a large, darkened front room. Heavy green velvet drapes were pulled across the windows beneath sweeping swags of the same green velvet, edged by gold braid and tassels. The air was damp and musty, age and dust fighting for their rightful place upon every ornament and fixture in the room.

The three of us were invited to take a seat, so I chose to stay close to my Grandmother. We sat in the biggest, most plumptious sofa I had ever seen. It gathered me up into its grey velvetiness, sinking ever down and down into the voluminous interior, surrounding me with huge damask cushions that smelt of old cat.

'Oh, what a wonderful surprise. How lovely to see you Auntie Beatie, it's been an absolute age.'

I heard her long before I was able to see her, due to my being trapped within the bowels of the sofa, both of my legs pointing upward toward the ornate plastered ceiling rose. Her voice sweet and pretty, each word landing gently upon the ear, light and beautiful as a butterfly.

Peering over my still upturned feet, she looked down at me with a very amused look upon her face.

'And who may this handsome young man be?'

Mad Masie

'I really don't know why he's acting so silly,' said Grandmother, suddenly pulling me forward. 'Sit up and stop showing off, you silly boy. Wherever are your manners?'

Grandmother's admonishments were whirling like a storm inside my head until I heard words that clearly said: 'Now go and give both your Aunties a hug and kiss and say hello. I don't think they have ever met you before, so introduce yourself properly.'

At that moment there was very little of me that wasn't burning. My tongue was unable to form any audible sound, let alone properly formed words. Struggling to break free from the sofa, I was finally able to stand before both ladies like a captured prisoner.

The next few moments of my life were sheer, giddy gobbledygook, a pitifully inadequate explanation of who I was and questions related to where I lived with my Mother. I could still taste Auntie Carrie's soft paper cheek where a dusting of powderpuff and rouge, reminiscent of Grandmother's bedroom, was tickling my nose. The very next moment, Masie had clutched me to her bosom, holding me tight for what felt like a lifetime until finally releasing me by kissing me loudly on my forehead.

Now Masie was standing before me, one hand on her hip, the other elegantly holding a long cigarette holder. She wore shoulder length auburn hair in a curly bob, glistening in folds and waves like fire. Unbelievably, I had never seen a woman dressed in trousers. She was wearing a Prince of Wales check pattern, together with a pink silk shirt and dangling cufflinks, the ensemble complimented with a loosely knotted black tie. She looked stunning to my very young naïve eyes, like a film star who had just walked out from a poster on the Royalty Cinema in Cowes.

'Beatie, you will all stay for luncheon?' asked Aunt Carrie, pausing a second for an acceptance.

'That'll be lovely,' interjected Bert. 'Save us from having to do a roast.'

Aunt Carrie turned to face Bert with a look that could have soured milk.

'No! I'm afraid that will not be possible, Bert. Masie will make sandwiches and hot tea for you and Harry which can be eaten in the garden whilst *you both* complete the clearing up.'

Masie, meanwhile, was blowing the most perfect smoke rings into the air. I watched fascinated as the rings followed each other, spiralling one way and then another, coming to a smoky rest across the ceiling. She now lazed in a large comfy armchair, her long legs stretched out, resting on a leather-bound footstool.

'Ham and cheese do you both?' she called from her reclination. 'With some of my homemade apple chutney?'

Bert nodded an agreement. His disconsolate expression broke into half a smile as he rose slowly from the comfort of the sofa, clearly in no hurry to tell Harry the news that they would be enjoying a working lunch of sandwiches and tea in the garden.

I had noted with interest that Aunt Carrie had referred to lunch as 'luncheon', which seemed to imply a formality and procedure the manner of which I knew not. I was aware that I was trepidatious, as Aunt Carrie did not look at all like a lady who would take "Oh, no, I'm sorry I don't like that". I prayed that whatever was to be set before us was within my limited range of acceptable food.

Eventually, with help from Grandmother, Masie and Aunt Carrie announced that luncheon was served. It had been arranged upon the largest dining table I had ever seen. There was a large china tureen of gazpacho soup, salad, smoked salmon, cold cooked salmon en croute, a bowl of buttered new potatoes, fresh home-produced asparagus, a large platter of crusty homemade bread, together with an assortment of olives and various cheeses in balsamic. A bottle of Riesling complemented the setting. I was offered a fizzing glass of American Soda.

So far, my young life's experiences of food were at very best limited; I had no knowledge whatsoever of most the food upon the table. Spaghetti in tomato sauce from a tin, served hot from a saucepan and placed on a piece of buttered toast was the only adventure into the world of gourmet I had ever undertaken.

To my everlasting gratitude, Masie had decided to sit beside me and immediately sensed my ineptitude – from my first sight of the odd-looking cutlery to hearing that not only did the soup have a strange name, a name that sounded foreign, but it was to be served cold. My Grandmother was not one who suffered fools gladly, nor was she one to be embarrassed by children – especially when she was in the company of her friends. She insisted in a very strict tone that I was to show my manners and to ensure that I would try a little of everything. The array of food and patterned china set before me began to blur, everything on the table began dancing and my mind was swimming as my ineptitude took hold. Yet I was aware of a sweet gentle voice breaking through the fog of blind panic which had such a tight grip me.

'This afternoon,' whispered Masie loudly so all could hear, 'after of course we have all finished eating and if your Grandmother has no objections, how would you like to accompany me and go for a ride on my motorbike? Sandown perhaps or—'

Both my Grandmother and Aunt Carrie immediately began to protest, interrupting each other as they did so. Masie bade them to desist by placing her forefinger to her lips.

'I'm sure this young man is going to be the very model of a good boy in order to win an afternoon on a motorbike. And if you are very good and please both Beatie and my dear Mother I may even show you how to ride a motorbike safely around the paddock and will be more than happy to finish up as soon as he can. Now what can I tempt you with?'

Smiling, she winked at me and began lightly spreading Brussels pâté onto a piece of crusty bread and overlaid it with a slice of smoked salmon, placing it upon a side plate with capers and pickles and a thin slice of cheddar cheese. She then cut an equally thin slice of the salmon en croute.

'I'm going to have exactly the same as you,' she said, quickly serving the same food once again onto another plate, 'and if I finish before you manage to finish I'm going to stay in this afternoon and knit, but should you finish before me then and only then will we go for a short ride over the Downs on the motorbike.'

'If I finish before you,' I blurted, my mouth already full of bread and pickle, 'can I still have a ride on your motorbike in the paddock and will you still show me how to ride it?'

Nodding in agreement and with a wave of her hand signalling me to get on with matter in hand, she began to eat heartily and with obvious intent to win her bet.

'Oh I almost forgot afters, we have to eat a slice of Beatie's apple pie which she has kindly given us,' she winked at my Grandmother, who was shaking her head in head in amusement, 'and not forgetting a big dollop of custard.'

It was almost as though she knew I loathed custard. But not today. Today I shall overcome.

Masie continued her encouragement by gently teasing and coaxing me through the luncheon and after a few faltering stumbles, coughs and splutters I managed to reach the dessert course – not forgetting the thick, gelatinous dollops of custard. Unbelievably, the meal was at an end.

My Grandmother had agreed that I had been both well-mannered and had eaten a sufficiency which had both pleased her and our hosts. She then gave me dubious leave of the table and told me to go into the garden and talk to my Uncles whilst the ladies wanted to discuss something urgent and important with Maisie.

After all she wasn't called Mad for nothing…

Both of my Uncles had enjoyed their ham and cheese sandwiches and Maisie had also taken out apple pie to them, but they were still grumbling about their lot in life.

'Not bloody good enough to eat at Lady Muck's table, we're just the bloody hoi polloi,' hissed Uncle Harry under his breath. 'Only good enough to clear up after bloody Barmy Drawers finished burning down half of Northwood. She could've burnt the whole ruddy street down and that's a fact.'

Bert nodded in agreement between mouthfuls of apple pie as Harry threw down another heap of charred timber in a clatter onto the ground.

'She's going to kill herself one day if she's not ruddy careful,' continued Uncle Harry, shaking his head in despair. 'Do you know Bert, she was by all accounts dancing around the bloody garden last night in her nightdress. It was about bloody midnight before they realised the ruddy shed was ablaze.'

'What started the fire off, do we know?'

'She kept a spare Jerry can of petrol in there for her bloody motorbike or some such, then she only goes and leaves a fag burning on the bench in that bloody fancy cigarette holder thingy she uses, next bloody minute *whoompff!*'

Bert sighed deeply and then took a last long swig of tea. He began rubbing his chin thoughtfully before saying, 'She reminds me of that mad dancer girl, you know what'shername, the mad bugger who got herself killed when her bloody scarf got caught up in the car's wheel.'

'That was Isadora Duncan,' said Harry. 'You're right there, she was as mad as a hatter too. They all come out of the same box, daft as bloody March Hares the whole lot of them. I've told you before, they're what they call the bloody crème de la crème.'

'Oh, I do love it when you speak in French, Harry,' said Bert, before bursting into a peel of camp laughter.

Douglas Dragonfly

Standing at the open French Window, Masie was waving excitedly and calling out to me to come in quickly. Shouting goodbye, I left my Uncles and ran as fast as I could towards the house and looking quickly back, I gave my Uncles a last wave. Bert was busying himself filling his pipe whilst Harry resigned himself once again to his task of clearing up the fire damage.

I followed Masie, who was dressed in motorcyclist black leathers, through the house. We found my Grandmother and Aunt Carrie standing inside the open garage doors, both looking with disdain at a shiny black motorcycle which was stood at a jaunty angle upon its stand.

'It's a Douglas Dragonfly,' said Maisie proudly, 'it's marvellous and so very nippy and—'

Her words were cut off by her Mother, who warned her once again of excessive and needless speed and to be very much aware that she was responsible for the care, *the very special care*, of her pillion passenger. She repeated her warnings again and again, and paying deference to my Grandmother who was stood beside her, tapped her arm reassuringly. My Grandmother looked on and began wringing her hands and twitching a nervous smile of agreement at Carrie.

'Beatie, please be assured,' said Aunt Carrie, sounding not unlike Jean Brodie, 'Masie will not, I repeat *will not* be taking him to Sandown or Newport or any other such place, but instead she will be going only a mile or so down the road to Northwood Church. She is going to lay some flowers from the garden on sweet Ernest's grave.' Gripping my Grandmother's hand, who was wiping away a tear, she smiled kindly and added: 'A special place you know well and love, Beatie.'

Masie, as well as finding me a large of pair goggles, had found an extra warm jumper, mustard coloured with black stripes, a tight, bright yellow woolly hat, and I had wound around my neck her cosy black knitted scarf. I must have looked reminiscent of a rather large bumblebee when finally I was seated pillion behind her, holding a bunch of flowers that she had given me which were intended to be laid upon the grave of my Grandfather. Moments later, Masie kicked the machine roaring, spitting angrily, noisily firing into life. Standing astride of the motorcycle for balance and turning her head back, she shouted at me over the noise of the engine.

'Hang on tight to me sweetheart and remember to lean over when I lean. I've promised Mother and your Gran we will go to Northwood Church but there's nothing stopping us going the long way on the way back – it'll be fun.'

Less than one minute later we were roaring loudly over the Newport Road until we had reached Church Road, heading for The Church of St. John the Baptist at Northwood.

A cold blustering squall had blown up somewhere out over the Solent, darkening the summer sky with curtains of lashing rain. It was of little comfort that I was dressed in woollen clothes from head to foot, as they were soaked through by the rainstorm. Even my goggles had, after a short while, filled with rainwater. Masie had slewed us to a standstill and leaned her motorbike irreverently beside the lychgate, which opened into the small, garlanded cemetery with numerous weathered headstones and memoriam standing every which way.

Although it had only taken minutes from leaving Oxford Street to arriving at Northwood Church, we were nonetheless desperate to fulfil our mission of laying our bunch of flowers against the headstone of my Grandfather, Ernest Samuel Ralfs. I had kept tight hold of them beneath my jumper, but due to the wind and rain and my enthusiastic safekeeping, sadly there was very little left of the floral bouquet when I extracted the dejected and broken stems, petals and leaves.

'Oh my good God!' exclaimed Masie, clasping her hand over her mouth. 'I think you've buggered the posy of flowers and that's a fact.'

We immediately exchanged a glance one to another and then back to the heap of broken foliage, a carnage of floribunda, that I was attempting to reassemble into some sort of bouquet worthy of reverential respect for my Grandfather. Shock, rain, and graveyards are possibly still to this day a guaranteed recipe for laughter.

I stood on the church path holding no more than a handful of drooping stalks whilst Masie, almost in hysterics, was leaning for support against a stone archangel, his arms outstretched to heaven as though to escape our disrespectful behaviour. By now, the rain was relentless and we both ran towards the church, taking shelter beneath the front portico entrance. Within this arched portal, upon all windowsills, were as many as six vases full of beautiful flowers, the colour of these lovely bouquets matching every bit that of the stunning colours that shone through from the stained-glass windows.

'My Mother and Father were married here at this church,' said Masie.

'When was that?' I asked.

'T'was in the dawn of time my dear,' she mused, 'when all the world was lovely and all the skies were blue. T'was when all the beasts could sing my dear; they could sing as sweet as any bird.'

Her words trailed off as she suddenly outstretched her arm and snatched a bunch of flowers from a vase. She laughed, spinning out onto the stone pathway, leaping and dancing into the open graveyard.

'Hello, can I be of any help, are you wishing to visit the church? I'm afraid there is no one here at the moment,' – the lady stopped for a moment mid-sentence and watched Masie take yet another mighty grand jeté – 'besides the vicar.'

The quivering voice belonged to a rather frail looking lady dressed in a grey plastic pac-a-mac and a bright multicoloured headscarf, struggling to carry a basket of flowers over her arm. Masie froze mid-flight, coming to a standstill between the grey headstones. She was immediately the personification of calm and control. It was as though a mere second or so prior the ballet in the rain had not happened.

'Good afternoon,' said Masie, smiling sweetly and gesturing a sweeping arm movement in my direction, 'we are looking for Ernest Samuel Ralfs.'

'I'm sorry,' said the lady, 'I'm not sure I can help, there's no one here but me.'

'Mr Ernest Samuel Ralfs is in the ground here at Northwood Church,' clipped Masie, 'he is laid amongst all these other souls at rest.' Lowering her head demurely, she said quietly: 'And we so wish to find him so that we may lay these flowers against his graveside.'

'He was my Grandfather,' I exclaimed, beaming at the lady, who was clearly flummoxed. 'He fought in the First World War and got wounded and medals.'

'Oh, I think I know what you need. There is a register here somewhere abouts,' said the lady and began searching through the dusty piles of hymn books and other church paraphernalia that was packed away in boxes in the corner of the dark vestry.

It had stopped raining, the squall had followed the river down to Newport, leaving the old cemetery glistening and bejewelled. The lady emerged blinking into sunshine waving a red ledger above her head.

'I think we'll find who you are looking for in here,' she shouted triumphantly, peering at us over her gold wire spectacles. 'What year was he interned?'

I slowly shook my head; I had no idea.

'Oh golly so sorry we have really no idea,' said Masie ruefully.

The lady introduced herself as Mrs Turner, the vicar's wife. After a brief search of her ledger, she was able to identify the burial plot's position and after a short walk up and down rows of headstones we duly arrived at the one with the correct inscription. It was so overgrown and weathered it was difficult to read. Mrs Turner said a short prayer over my Grandfather's grave as we laid our purloined flowers reverently beside the headstone.

'I bet you did not know that your Grandmother Beatie and your Grandfather Ernest were married here at Northwood Church too,' said Masie, as she was struggling to kick the bike into life.

'What!' I exclaimed. I had only this very day found out that he was buried at Northwood Church and now I had discovered that my Grandmother and Grandfather were married here as well.

Masie cupped one hand to the side of her mouth, as though she was about tell me a secret.

'That's not all,' she whispered, 'Ernest Samuel had been married a year or so before to some other woman here at the same church.'

My eyes were wide agog, my mouth wide agape. How much more to know of my family could there be?

'Never ever in your life stop reading'

We set off in a flurry of fury as the Douglas Dragonfly zoomed out from the hallowed portal of the lychgate from where Masie had kicked life into its noisy 350cc engine. We appeared from a skid through a plume of muddy water up to the main Newport Road; I don't think I could have been any wetter if I had swum.

Masie, true to her word, had decided she most definitely was going to take the longest way home. Cowes and Gurnard blurred past as I clung on to her for dear life, leaning one way and then another as rain like cold bullets peppered me from head to foot. We hurtled toward Thorness, down the straight Old Rew Street onto Hillis Corner until we reached Forest Road, past Porchfield, then finally heading back home as we sped up Newport Road from Hunny Hill. I was somewhat relieved when we finally arrived, screeching to a standstill outside the garden gate of Masie's home. Oh, the joy to be once again in the quiet sanctuary of Oxford Street. I was, however, proud of the fact that I had completed my baptism of fire by motorcycle, riding pillion with Mad Masie as she raced the Douglas Dragonfly through squalling rain, wind and storm. Yes indeed, Mad Masie was without a doubt my new best friend and as far as my own family was concerned, the font of all knowledge.

Grandmother and Aunt Carrie were both delighted and no doubt relieved to see us both as they sat together in the dimly lit front room, enjoying tea and cake. Both my old Uncles had completed their tasks in the garden and were now, by way of a reward, reading the papers and enjoying a small measure of whisky. They sat, relaxing comfortably in large, cushioned rattan chairs in the bright conservatory.

My alighting from the pillion seat of the motorbike and straddle-waddle-walking to the house must have been a sight for sore eyes. Woollen clothes for motorcyclists in the rain is not to be recommended. What had been reminiscent of a happy bumblebee now resembled a very wet and unhappy caterpillar. My Grandmother had borrowed some very odd items of dry clothing from Aunt Carrie which smelt of camphor and must. Aunt Carrie insisted that they once belonged to a young nephew of hers that had no further need of them, as he had died of diphtheria some years previous.

'They will do until we get home this evening,' hissed Grandmother under her breath, 'and be sure you give yourself a good rub down.'

The small hand towel was as rough as tree bark and once again imbued with the strange unpleasant odour of camphor and must.

'Oh my oh goodness...' said Masie, partially smiling as she quickly placed a hand over her mouth to stifle a giggle, 'you look the very image of Little Lord Fauntleroy.'

This time her stifled giggle had burst free, developing into what can only be best described as a belly laugh. She saw my look of ignorant disbelieving. I neither knew what I looked like nor for that matter who Little Lord Fauntleroy was.

'Where on Earth did those clothes come from? Did Mother give them to you? Oh good God in Heaven she has only gifted you poor dead Derek's Sunday best! He died of diphtheria do you know when I was just a little girl. He died – they say he was in a bit of state bless him – here at this house in my bedroom.' She pointed her finger to the ceiling. 'Poor thing he had always been a very unlucky child so my Mother tells me. Evidently he was my second cousin as indeed was his sister Hettie of course she died in Switzerland of consumption.'

The early evening watery sunlight beamed through the windows of the comfortable tumble of the family room in long dusty shafts as we sat talking together. I had never in my life had a grown-up friend, but I believed I had found such a one in

Masie. As well as being mad, Masie was so interesting and profound. I could hang on her every word forever.

'I am so awfully sorry lovie I know that I promised but it seems we have no time for your motorbike lesson. Besides the weather is so foul and the grass in the paddock is so very wet and so very slippery.'

I told her not to worry, assuring her that today's experience had left a lasting impression on me. A chill ran down my spine as I brought to mind some of the twists and turns at what felt well over a million miles an hour. Although I didn't go into the detail pertaining to the fact it was highly unlikely that I would ever forget my first experience on a motorbike.

Masie smiled at me sweetly, saying that she was sure there would be other times and opportunities.

'Yes indeed,' I nodded a lie. I knew at that moment that motorcycles and myself would never grow to have the very truest of alliances. (Many years later, I purchased my first and last motorcycle – a Yamaha 250cc – and spent some time flying through the air and spinning through hedge backs. I am certain in the knowledge that I pushed it back home as many miles as I ever rode it.)

I recalled watching Masie dancing in the rain, gracefully floating between the grey sombre headstones in the cemetery. She explained that she had sudden impulses that demanded she free her spirit and endeavour to vie with nature and all elements. She went on to say it was the same with writing and poetry, and asked me if I was interested in reading and poetry.

I enthusiastically nodded another lie.

'Then tell me,' she said, sweetly smiling broadly down into my face, 'who is your most favoured poet and what is your most treasured book?'

I wondered if she was able to feel the intense heat from my cheeks. I most certainly could.

'I don't remember,' I stammered. I wanted to burst into tears. What she must think of me? Not so much for being a numbskull, but far worse – a dishonest numbskull.

Masie took my hand in hers and led me over to a massive wall of books on the far side of the room. She stood scanning the shelves for a moment before removing two. She flicked through the pages and after a short while handed them to me saying, as her eyes pierced into mine, 'Promise me you will read these books.'

The two books she had given me were *The Song of Hiawatha* by Henry Wadsworth Longfellow and *Poems* by John Masefield, the Poet Laureate.

'Yes,' I said, as honestly and sincerely as I could, with yet another enthusiastic nodding of my head.

'Never ever in your life stop reading,' she said in the closest I had ever heard her scold me. 'Reading and particularly reading poetry is like opening a new box of paints onto a new and imaginary world. Read each word slowly, savour it and enjoy the sound of it. Give it a colour.'

She went on to explain freedom of expression and imagination, particularly when she was able to dance and move without inhibitions. She had never been given the opportunity to be able to study the discipline or the art of dance, or ever received lessons.

Masie quivered with passion as she explained the very first time that she had felt the raw Mother Earth beneath her naked feet. That moment had fired her forever into the free movement of dance and expression. Detailing the freedom and utter beauty of movement to its nearest equivalent, she likened it to what a bird must feel each time it launches itself from a branch.

'It's such a pity it was not the finest of days today because sometimes I pop off over to Sandown in order to fly Mr Peter's aeroplane,' she added.

She was aware of my open mouth and tapped my arm to regain my attention.

'I really do find that far less dangerous an undertaking than riding the Douglas Dragonfly at speed in the rain,' she giggled. 'Once again and at the risk of boring you silly I just love both the power and the strength of the air turbulence, but most of all I simply adore the sheer freedom beneath my wings as I peer at our wonderful world slowly unfolding beneath me.'

My words failed me.

My Grandmother and Aunt Carrie entered the room, followed by my Uncles. My Grandmother informed me that it was time for us all to take our leave and to be sure to thank both Aunt Carrie and Masie for a wonderful day. I really didn't want the day to end; every word that Masie had told me was resonating in my head, my mind was spinning, it was alive with wonder and afire with new and as yet undiscovered ideas.

We all began to gather outside on Oxford Street in order to say our farewells as we hugged and kissed.

Aunt Carrie felt frail and breakable and still smelt musty. She was antiqued and very definitely of another bygone time.

My Uncles had waddled out in front, carrying a large straw basket full of greengages between them. They had picked them earlier that afternoon during the rain.

I stood for a moment, hugging Masie and thanking her for the most memorable day I thought I had ever had. I promised her once again that I would read the books that she had given me.

Masie bent forward and kissed me loudly on both cheeks and then proceeded to punch me playfully on my arm. She began to cry as she reiterated, through soft sobs of joyous affection, her promise that we would see each other very soon.

I watched my two old Uncles toddle lovingly off home towards Wyatts Lane, both happy that Aunt Carrie had paid them handsomely for their hard work with a brand new, crisp, white five-pound note and the greengages.

The memory of Aunt Carrie and Mad Masie leaning over their garden gate, waving us all a fond farewell whilst silhouetted by the early evening sun, has remained with me all of my life as though it was only yesterday.

With the exception of my Grandmother, I never saw any one of them again.

Within three years, both of my dear Uncles had died. Bert sadly following his lifelong friend Harry within two months.

The following year, Aunt Carrie died peacefully in her sleep.

My wonderful Grandmother, whilst taking up an invitation to visit Australia to stay with her eldest daughter and her family, died of a heart attack on board the cruise ship SS Canberra and was buried at sea.

Masie, so rumour has it, moved to Canada some time during the early sixties. By my best calculations she would now be enjoying her ninety-sixth year. It certainly would not surprise me if she was still dancing and taking the odd flight into the blue.

A Field Walk to Folly

Down across the grasslands swaying
Beside the Medina's hush of morning
Growing there in reed and rushes
Round brown mice heart a-beating
Scatter beneath the grasslands swaying
Beside the Medina's lap and ripple
Where wings of fairies come a-spinning
Weave golden webs from tree to tree
Come them dressed in oak and apple
Come them dressed in leaf and blossom
Over the grasslands gently swaying
Brushed them night all silver shining
Shining like Medina's water dancing
Upon the rhythm of its mystic water
To the furthest wooded green glade
Where wild crab apple red as ruby
Ruby like a blood red flower
Over the grasslands gently swaying
Beside the Medina's hush of morning

In a Pear Tree

During the long, hot, weekend afternoons of August 1955, I could be found at Tic's in Adelaide Grove. It was an opportunity to go and visit my Father who in turn spent his time with Tic, his Father, and therefore we passed like ships in the night. My Father and Tic spent most of their weekends patiently awaiting the return home of Tic's racing pigeons from France or Spain.

The birds would be released earlier that day and Tic would estimate that they could fly approximately at an average of sixty-five miles per hour. Sometimes, if the wind was blowing in the right direction and they were able to fly high enough, they could reach even faster speeds. Unfortunately, high winds or storms would often blow the pigeons far off course over the Channel, exhausting them – or worse, they would fall prey to hawks or large sea birds.

I would grow quickly bored of constantly craning my neck, searching the skyline awaiting the first sight of a returning bird. I was always much happier to wander away into the garden or search the contents of Tic's old shed which was always full of stored apples, tied hanging strings of onions and other garden produce. There was also a weird collection of old military relics, tin helmets, large brass cannon shells and gas masks. Once, I even found an old rusty bayonet.

I also loved to climb the many tall old fruit trees which edged the raggedy pathway that led for two hundred yards or so to the very top of the garden, which was where Tic housed chickens and his highly prized pigeons. The long line of old apple, plum and pear trees, many of which had never seen a pruning saw, were nonetheless almost always adorned heavily with fruit.

There was one particular pear tree, a special tree, that was my most favourite to climb: a William's. I had been told by Tic that it was even older than him. It was ideal for climbing and particularly if you wanted to be alone or intended to hide away from the world. Its trunk was dried and gnarled with a spreading thicket of branches and at this time of year it was always heavily laden with golden, fat juicy pears.

It was another racing Saturday on a very hot afternoon, the sky a clear azure blue. Both Tic and my Father were fractious to say the least. They were being frustrated by Tic's champion red checker, who had returned in a very good time, but decided to tease them both. No matter how much they would coo and rattle the corn tin to entice her down to the loft, it seemed she was happier flying in flashes of iridescence, circling high above their heads.

'It's still a bloody good time if she comes down even now,' said my Father checking his watch. 'Poor little bugger, coming all the way here from Bordeaux, you'd think she'd be ready for a good feed.'

Tic nodded, hissing an almost indecipherable whispered agreement. Both men continued to coo and rattle, occasionally looking up and squinting into the sun for a glimpse of the next bird to come spiralling down to hopefully alight onto a small platform, pecking greedily at the scattered corn tempter in front of the bird's entrance which was a system of one-way curtains of tiny vertical bars.

What idiosyncrasies or skills one needed to adopt to ensure the speedy official timing of a reluctant champion homing pigeon was being both demonstrated and passionately discussed loudly by Tic and my Father.

Breathing heavily and sweeping the sweat from her brow through her silver hair, Grandmother Hilda walked slowly over from the other side of the garden, closer to where I was sat above in the pear tree. She was moving through the canes of fruit as loud expletives rent the air, flicking away warring wasps which had been particularly bothersome this summer. The perfume of loganberries, purple, plump and sweeter than honey, imbued the summer air, rising and mingling with the sweetness of the ripe pears. Grandmother Hilda placed the loganberries carefully into a large wicker basket that already contained raspberries and green figs. From my position in the tree, I could hear her huffing and puffing, determined in her husbandry of fruit harvesting, as now she straddled over large green leaves as she pulled at the long tender pink stalks of rhubarb.

My dreamlike state of mind was abruptly aware of my Father's voice loudly alerting Tic to the fact that the Miele cock was overhead, immediately followed by yet another two homecoming birds. All this excitement was followed by a raucous chorus of cooing and a rattling clash of corn tins. Despite all that was happening, I heard my Father calling out my name loudly from where he was stood with Tic at the pigeon loft. The very next moment he was standing beneath the pear tree in which I was sat, asking Grandmother Hilda if she knew where I was.

'I never ever see the little sod for bloody weeks and then when you need the little bugger he's nowhere to be bloody found,' ruefully sighed my Father.

'Last time I saw your nipper he was nosing about in our shed again. If Tic catches him, he'll clip his bloody ear and no mistake,' said Hilda stingingly, as she slashed the air against another insistent wasp. 'I'm going down home with this basket, if I see him, I'll tell him you wants him. Probably still in our bloody shed poking about.'

Hilda continued to hiss dismissive expletives at the wasps that were intent on exploiting her summer basket of freshly picked fruit.

'Bugger's always disappearing when you need him,' shouted back my Father. 'If you see him, tell him I want him to nip over the road for some fags and a bottle of Mews and Langton from

Miss Fry's fridge for Tic. When you find the little bugger tell him to hurry up about it and to take that ten-bob note on the sideboard down home.' Then he added as an afterthought: 'And tell him not to lose the bloody change.'

I could see my Father's head, his blond curls glinting golden in the bright sunshine – save that is for a shining pink balding pate which was glistening immediately below me. To this day I shall never know what it was that possessed me, but as my Father stood, his hands upon his hips, shouting his instructions to Grandmother Hilda, I called out his name…

I hadn't deliberately picked the fattest, yellow, over-ripe pear, which unbeknownst to me was full of happily feasting wasps within. It was just the first pear to come to hand.

I saw the pink patch shining up at me, a target through the gold of his curls, and dropped the pear and all of its busy contents. It fell soundlessly through the warm air travelling the short distance liken to a bomb upon a target, exploding on impact upon my Father's head. The heavy wet sound of the bursting pear, a *splat* that sent sticky juices and angry wasps flying in all directions, was closely followed my Father crying out as though he'd been struck on his head by a cricket ball.

Shouting loudly, he grasped and held onto his head, repeatedly running in half-crazed circles around the old pear tree, closely followed by a growing number of very incensed wasps.

What followed over that long hot lazy August afternoon in Tic's garden was a blur, most of the detail thankfully lost to the annals of memory and time. Suffice to say that for the greater part of that afternoon and into the early evening I had locked myself in the outside yard lavatory, better described as a midden. Despite the stench I refused to open the door, afraid to face my Father until his wrath had completely subsided. Eventually I plucked up the courage to pull the slide-bolt and open the door of the reeking hellhole and face my Father, who had been patiently waiting close by.

I recall a short but earnest discussion with my him, together with the hot stinging tingle radiating from my backside, as I walked slowly home that evening to Kent House where my Mother was awaiting me.

How did such a moment of sheer madness ever happen? It is a question I am unable to answer, the whole episode to this day remains a complete and utter mystery. My blood still runs cold even now when my memory journeys back to that rash moment. It has been many a long year since I was sat with my legs a-dangling down over the branches of the old pear tree in Tic's garden in East Cowes.

Dusk was deciding the close of day, all was at peace once again. The wasps, tired of their aggressive pursuit, had retired to their nest. Tic's pigeons had all safely returned, save one rebellious champion red checker who was happy to remain perched on the highest pinnacle of Grange Road School.

Gypsy Girl

Summer Funfair, Westwood Park, 1955

Long legs spangle, dangle
In her garnet red patent leather shoes
With shining silver buckle O's
Ruby down her henna hair
Comes tumbling curling and dancing
Over her shoulders of alabaster
Her words
Oh! to hear her words
Her words smile you a thousand kisses
Words swimming in deep sapphire oceans
Poetry painted in broad stokes of rainbow
Words that splash across a stretched white canvas
Ascend like coloured balloons
Words that carry her dreaming upon the wind
Mesmerized, we are caught within her emerald gaze
Held spellbound

She was just a darkly gypsy girl
No frills no fancy
A pretty girl with flowers in her hair
A fairground girl
Poppy red and red again, red cherry lips
Sweet dip me do gingerbread girl
Razzle-dazzle
Diamond dancing girl
Dancing in her red, red shoes

The Initiation

For as long as I could remember, in the top field adjacent to the Bommy Building, was a fallen sycamore tree. It lay in a tangled profusion from root bowl to topmost bough and was at least sixty feet in length. It had long since lost its outer bark and many of the broken branches had rotted away from the main trunk, which spanned the breadth of the small field like a bridge. The only vegetation still existing in the field was a plethora of twisted, prickly thistle, which wound itself in hardy abundance, together with stinging nettles and wild brambles that grew up through the tree, to adorn the still mighty trunk in a green leafy mantle.

Two of my friends, Michael Brinton and Philip Hunt, were boys that had, in addition to being notorious and imaginative storytellers, always enjoyed being sadistically creative. Whilst stealing birds' eggs, catching fish and newts may have been considered quite normal when I was a boy, pulling the wings from butterflies most certainly was not.

As usual, some of us – Sherf, Alan Hick, Robert Mullet and his cousin John Riddell – had met at the old green bench seat which was situated beside the bus stop across the road from Kent House. Michael was very animated and excited as he outlined the details of a grisly dare that both Philip and he had undertaken, allegedly, only minutes before we had all arrived. Each moment of their evident success lit up their faces almost to the point of drooling. It seemed we had all just missed it by minutes.

The small field immediately behind the bench had been given over to a couple of families of grubbing pigs. For several years the greater part of the field had been rooted out and snorted over until hardly a blade of grass grew, save for the huge, old fallen sycamore that laid across the field almost corner to corner. To gain access to the fallen tree was reasonably easy from the York Avenue side. It was a simple matter of climbing over the fence and pulling yourself up through the mass of thick twisted roots, where you were then able to walk, albeit carefully, along the whole length of trunk. On the left-hand side of the tree was the small piggery field of Warner's Farm, containing three pigsties housing many piglets, six sows, and the biggest and most bad-tempered old boar pig I had ever seen in my life. This big boar, unlike the others, was a bit of a loner. His harem was more than happy, when not asleep, to roll and snuffle for whatever they were able to grub up within the rich dark ooze that surrounded them and would sometimes take the opportunity to wallow in the mud pools gifted to them by recent summer rain. As the fallen sycamore tree served the purpose of a stock-proof division, lying as it did across the breadth of the field, everything to the right-hand side of the tree remained verdant and lush and untouched by the pigs.

Disbelief and scepticism were written across our faces as Mike and Phil finished describing what they had accomplished earlier that morning: the two of them defying certain death by taking on the raging boar and stinging his balls with nettles.

'Bugger off! You never did anything of the kind,' said Sherf. 'That old bastard would have had you both for breakfast.'

'Bloody killed you more like, ripped you apart with his fangs,' said John, grinning from ear to ear in obvious disbelief.

'Bloody tusks you mean, not fangs, you daft bugger,' chastised his cousin Robert. 'He's a bloody boar, not a python.'

'Sounds like a lot of bullshit to me, Sherf,' said Hicks.

'Pigshit more like,' laughed Robert. 'That big bugger can turn on a sixpence when he's a mind to, I've seen him when he's been chasing them other big buggers off.'

Hicks pointed a trembling finger at the old boar who was

stood facing him with what he felt sure were menacing eyes, unblinking and glowering liken to tiny red-hot coals.

Robert, who was always the most introspective and thoughtful amongst us, pointed at the two boys' feet.

'There's not a lot of dirt on your plimsoles. Or your hands for that matter. Both of you buggers would be covered in pig shit from head to foot if you had really been in there.'

Both Mike and Phil had sworn on their lives, crossed their hearts and hoped to die should they not be telling the truth. They alleged they had wrapped their hands with dock leaves and pulled a bunch of stinging nettles from beside the tree. Thus armed, they had continued quietly along the tree trunk and once they were at the bottom end had jumped, a matter of two or three feet, into the pig field.

Once in the field, ensuring that they were as quiet as possible, they had stealthily crept up on the old boar. When they were as close as they dared be, they had whipped his gigantic scrotum with the bunched nettles. When he turned on them both, roaring with pain and indignation, his gleaming tusks bared and ready to trample them underfoot, they had both escaped by running as fast as their legs would carry them back to the safety of the tree.

A chorus of objection, disbelief and expletives was followed by Sherf abruptly bringing matters to a head by saying, 'Okay, yeah, fair enough,' as he nodded an agreement in Phil's direction, which had the effect of bringing the noisy confrontation to a momentary close.

Sherf pointed to the pig field.

'Alright then, good idea,' he said. 'We all go in one at a time and flick him up the balls. But you and Mike can lead the way and show us how it's done.' He clapped his hands together. 'Come on you two, get yourselves sorted and get in the field.'

'Piss off!' said Hicks, who was still eyeballing the big boar. 'If you think I'm going in there you can bloody well think again.'

'Yeah, I hear what you say, but I still think you're going,' said Sherf, grinning from ear to ear as he placed his hand reassuringly upon Hicks's shoulder. 'You're too bloody windy for your own good, but don't you worry nipper, Gussy will be going in there with you.'

'What about you Sherf, when are you going in?' I asked.

'I'll be in there, don't you worry about that nipper,' said Sherf quietly, 'but what I was thinking is that Phil and Mike will show us how easy it's done first.'

'Bugger off! We've bloody well done it once haven't we!' objected Mike Brinton at the top of his voice, displaying his hands high in the air, back and front. 'If you buggers don't believe me, just look at my bloody hands, they're all red from where the nettles stung me through the dock leaves.'

'When they should be all covered in pig shit,' mused Robert.

'Bugger off Mullet, we've wiped it all off on the grass,' protested Mike.

All of us, eyebrows raised, regarded his remarks with amused disdain. Phil was just as vocally adamant that his previous encounters with all things porcine were and should be recognised as an achievement. He, like Mike, made much of displaying his hands as clear evidence of his accomplishment, which he also said were still red and throbbing as the result of being stung by nettles.

Sherf, impatient of both boys' continued resistance, suddenly and by way of friendly but meaningful persuasion, dead-legged Mike with so resounding a punch that we all heard the thump.

Mike's painful protests were to no avail, so Phil began pulling handfuls of dock leaves from the hedgerow, instructing him to wrap the cooling leaves tighter around both of his hands. The rest of us began to do likewise.

Reluctantly, Mike climbed over the old iron rail fence and balanced upon the fallen tree trunk, looking down with some trepidation upon the quietly feeding pigs.

As ever, Sherf had taken charge. He seemed to be taking great delight in preparing the rest of us, ensuring we were all adequately protected from stings by dock leaves, and with a helping hand over the fence and up to the tree trunk. We queued upon it, edging our way along and ready to jump into the field to face the savagery of the wild beast that awaited. Soon the small field was full of very nervous boys, together with a great number of very noisy and over-excited pigs.

The pigs, ever curious and having caught sight of us bearing garlands of foliage in our trembling hands, had decided that it must be feeding time. Just like dogs, pigs wag their tails when they are both pleased and excited, and the sows and piglets scampered forward squealing their delight. Such was their united joy, they all came running as one, vying to be the first for whatever juicy morsels were to hand. Both pigs and piglets were as fleetfooted as racehorses as they sped towards us.

We, unfortunately, were not quite as nimble or agile.

The Mire

Underfoot, the pigpen field was at best a sodden midden, but when one needed to retreat at speed back to the safety of the tree, the ground beneath became as slippery and dangerous as ice.

I was the first to falter, crashing down into the vile stench. Splaying out my arms and legs in the mud, I must have looked like a spatchcock chicken. My hapless downfall was closely followed by screams from Mike and Hicks as they both attempted to help each other to stand, whereupon they fell into the curdle of black mire again and again.

Robert and John had not ventured too far from the tree and were being pulled to safety by Sherf, who was as yet unscathed.

Unlike dogs, sows and piglets do not lick your face or jump up at you to show their adoration or pleasure. But pigs do push their slavering, snorting snouts hard and enquiringly into your body and face in their ever-desperate pursuit for food. Although the typical pig's bulk at first sight looks to be pallid and soft, this belies the nature of the beast; each one of the pigs was rough and tough, with bristling coarse hair which grew sharp and piercing as steel wool over their broad backs.

The rich and pungent stench of everything porcine drifted up into the still, warm air, leaving its odious stain on the early Sunday afternoon of that beautiful summer's day. Beneath the sun, all of us were slipping and sliding in every direction and making little or no progress whatsoever – still accompanied by a large group of relentless, excited and hungry pigs as they ran, snuffling and nipping at our heels.

'Come here, you big bastard,' screamed Phil, who was now determined at any cost to carry out his planned assault on the poor old boar. He began waving his bunch of wilting nettles madly in the air.

The colossus of a pig stood and looked back at him with a

blank disinterested expression, before snorting loudly, turning and slowly walking away. In his rage, Phil lost his footing, spinning in mid-air. He came crashing down into the rancid soft earth, his frail, thin form resembling a broken cranefly. With dung and all manner of disgusting detritus filling both his open mouth and nostrils, he slid, face first, through the black slime to a standstill against a couple of large sows, their tails wagging, seemingly delighted to accept whatever it was that he held in his clenched hands.

Mike, having fallen yet again, was also on his knees trying unsuccessfully to regain his balance. He was surrounded by a large group of shrieking piglets, delighted to have someone to play with that smelt so much like themselves. His khaki shorts were by now jet black and taking on the appearance of a shining leather skirt, both his pockets filled to the brim with slippery black slurry. Falling yet again, Mike plunged headlong into a wallow pig pool and for a second was completely submerged. He reappeared moments later, covered from head to foot in a greenish shimmering hue that sparkled and dripped iridescent beneath the sun. After countless crashes and splashes into the mire, we finally made our way back towards the safety of the tree.

With the aid of a long, broken, leafy branch, Sherf helped retrieve us one by one from our mud-sodden positions and onto the safety of the old sycamore's trunk. This was, he later explained, so that he didn't have to touch us. When he had first witnessed our distress (and more importantly, our collective inability to stand for any more than a few seconds), he had made an executive decision to stay put, as – he said – he was better equipped to help and stay guardian within the bastion of the fallen tree. Since we all stank like a cesspit, he suggested we should go home, get washed and changed and meet up again tomorrow.

The event, the raison d'être, the highlight of our day was to have been the stinging in the balls of the world's fiercest boar, the whipping nettles slashed unmercifully against the exposed and dangling pink scrotum. Sadly, the old boar had not figured at all. There had been no massive, dangle-down, pink hairy scrotum defiled by daring, swashbuckling boys. Instead, there had been nothing more than clumsy humiliation; retaliation of a kind by a group of his happy, grunting and loyal sows together with their excited, squealing offspring. That, and our inept inability to place one foot in front of the other without falling over and sliding uncontrollably through the stench and vile midden of the Warner's pig field, had won the day.

The massive bulk of the old boar, seemingly unperturbed and completely disinterested in the day's events in the kingdom of his piggery, was more than happy to abandon his tribe of noisy porkers, choosing instead to wander off to the furthest edge of the small field and ponder. Once there, the old boar spent his time peering through the open bars of the boundary iron fence, content to watch passers-by and those waiting at the bus stop for the Number 5 Southern Vectis to make its way slowly up York Avenue.

This was the summer of 1956 and my Mother was still very fragile from her recent illness, which meant that going home was not an option for me. Instead, I chose to leave the gang of boys, venturing over East Cowes Castle fields down to the shoreline of the Solent. How cool and clean the feeling of sea and shingle was between my toes, as I stood at Norris Castle Point. I was happy to spend the rest of the warm afternoon and early evening searching for crabs and shells, letting the Solent and the salt sea wash me and my clothes as best it could.

The Silver Birch Tree

Over down along meadowsweet and buttercup
Holy stones, *sanctum est,* above the quiet running river
Where long ago summers meet
Two lovers sat beneath a tree
Upon the long green bank above the quiet running river

Within the hush of Heaven's garden stands a tree
Beside Victoria's church above the quiet running river
Blue cranesbill twine the silver
Two lovers lay beneath a tree
Beneath the green canopy above the quiet running river

About the peeling silver bark sweet flowers grow
Rain, falling soft as light above the quiet running river
Their ashes forever dust to lie
Two lovers ever beneath a tree
Beside the green meadows above the quiet running river

My parents' ashes were scattered after a church service at St. Mildred's, Whippingham in 2007, beneath the leafy canopy of a silver birch. They had returned to this church to renew their wedding vows in the summer of 1992.

A Girl's Bike

It was not so much the getting to where you wanted to be on the island as the ability to return from where you had first started. So began and ended my first 'Round the Island Cycle Trip'.

A week or so before this travesty of events took place, Sherf, in his inimitable manner, had suggested that our small gang of York Avenue mates should circumvent the island on our bicycles.

'We could have a great laugh,' he began to expound, excitedly. 'It will be fantastic—'

'Carisbrook Castle might be good,' interrupted Mike Brinton, mid-spiel.

'Bugger off Mike,' snapped Sherf. 'Bloody Carisbrook. It's nowhere near far enough, it's only about seven miles.'

'*Only seven miles,*' withered Hicks, rolling his eyes to the heavens.

'Christ! You're a windy sod, Hicks,' clipped Sherf, returning his homily once again to us. 'I reckon around the island would be a doddle. The Needles, Freshwater or the Alum Bay area should take us about two hours, then straight down the Military Road from Freshwater down to St. Catherine's Point, another hour and a half.'

'Cycle around the sodding island?' said Robert questionably, pushing his hands through his hair. 'Do you have any idea just how far that is!'

'Course I do,' said Sherf, smiling now like a Cheshire Cat. 'It's only about sixty miles.'

Throughout the early evening his suggestions met with one objection after another until I piped up with my very valid interruption.

'Sorry old mate, but I'm out. Can't go, my bike is buggered. As you know, I've bent the forks when I crashed it last week.'

'I know that, Gussy. Don't you worry, I've got a spare bike all lined up for you.'

Sherf's spare bike! I could hardly contain my excitement; he was prepared to lend me *his* spare bike! Knowing his predilection for the very best in cycles, I just knew he would have something stylish and racy in mind.

'What sort of bike is the spare then?' I enquired eagerly.

'It's my sister's old Hercules Artisan, same as yours only it's a girl's bike. The Sturmey Archer gear change on the handlebar is buggered, but apart from that it's all right—'

'A bloody girl's bike!' I exploded in full voice, long before he could finish extolling the virtues of his sister June's bicycle.

All my friends knew of my despair at riding my Hercules Artisan for the last two years. Even though I had changed the handlebars and removed the mudguards, it remained a heavy, big, black, clodhopper of a bike. The safety of my bike was made worse due to an accident whereby I had bent the front forks excessively, so much so that I feared they may crack and collapse completely if ridden regularly. However, at that moment my friends took great delight in Sherf's choice of replacement for my trip around the island and continued throughout that early summer evening to tease me unmercifully. Que será, será.

As usual with Sherf, the idea of cycling around the island became a reality long before the end of the same evening. We all agreed to make the necessary arrangements and make ready for the following Saturday. An early morning start time of 7am was decided upon and we were all to bring at least ten shillings for spends and emergencies plus enough food and water to sustain us over the journey. Sherf and Robert had calculated that it would take us, allowing for food breaks, approximately ten hours, enabling our return safely to East Cowes to be no later than 6pm.

The route we finally agreed to take for our circumvention had been planned by Sherf's Father, Jock, who had taken the trouble to study his motoring atlas and revise the approximate mileage. It had been decided the journey would be advantaged by travelling west to east. Whether this was due to the sun or not was of no matter, as it turned out the day was grey and overcast, but nonetheless that was the direction we followed.

The early morning river mist chilled the air as I joined the small gathering of boys on bikes, my trusty iron steed gifted to me for the day by June Sherfield. Chilly, excited chatter combined with the sulphurous smell of egg sandwiches as they were being hurriedly packed into saddlebags, together with juices, water and pac-a-macs. Dressed for the occasion, we were an array of khaki shorts, old school shirts with frayed sleeves rolled up in defiant determination, with black plimsoles and dirty tennis shoes completing the sartorial elegance of our merry band. The only parent who had come to join to our gathering and wish us bon voyage was Mr Sherfield, who was waving his RAC road atlas in the air, busy giving us last minute advice on routes, all things directional, and re-enforcing our collective need to stay aware of the Highway Code (a publication not one of us had heard of).

The next minute we were pedalling as fast as we could down York Avenue and Skipper Elliot had rolled off a ream of penny tickets for our chain ferry crossing. As we stood waiting for the ferry I was tempted to open one of two boxed Lyons individual apple pies inside my saddlebag (packed by my Mother, together with the mandatory egg sandwiches, two apples and some jam doughnuts).

As the heavy black ramp of the chain ferry touched the west and to the astonishment and great amusement of my companions, I was just finishing my second sugared jam doughnut, having already demolished both pies. I brushed my sticky fingers down my shirt as we followed in noisy convoy down Medina Road, heading for the High Street and eventually out onto the Esplanade, passing the starting cannons of The Royal Yacht Squadron, ever onwards toward Gurnard.

This unaccustomed exertion was exacerbated by the tide being out, leaving a stench of drying out seaweed combining with something else even more nauseous leaking from the ancient sewage outlet spilling its evil detritus onto the exposed rocks.

Now, safely past Egypt Esplanade (interestingly, the Isle of Wight's most northerly point), we reached Gurnard in a fantastic time. From here, we decided to take the coastal path, which was off piste, insofar as it consisted of grass and beach path rather than a constructed road surface. Whilst the coastal pathway was reasonable, it certainly was not as easy to keep up a steady pace once we had started to go cross country. The field and grassed surface was very uneven and there were long stretches of sand and dune that made it necessary to carry or push our bikes.

We pressed on until we reached Thorness. It had taken much longer than we had anticipated, so we decided that we would leave the coastal path and pick up the old Whitehouse Road in Shalfleet, which would hopefully lead us down to the main Forest Road, which in turn would take us directly to Yarmouth, and by so doing we would easily have made up our lost time.

The noise of a front tyre puncture is hardly discernible. However, the cyclist is well aware of it and as I watched my front wheel wag uncontrollably front and left, I called out to those ahead that I needed help. I brought my bike to a halt and prodded the offending tyre with an investigatory finger. Hicks was the first to arrive, peering over his handlebars.

'Oh hell, Gus has got a puncture,' he yelled to the others as they returned one by one. 'I hope one of us has got a puncture repair kit.'

'None of you buggers were listening to my Dad this morning!' shouted Sherf and began listing the basic requirements we needed before undertaking this trip. '"*Have we all got puncture outfits?*"...

"Have we all got a working pump?"… "Have we all got some plasters and a bandage"…'

'Bugger off Sherf,' objected Mike, 'I hardly had any room in my saddlebag to start with, let alone all that stuff your Dad was going on about. I would have needed a bloody caravan!'

Taking a ring spanner and removing my front wheel, Sherf began to lever off the tyre, enabling him to carefully pull out the innertube. He unclipped my bicycle pump from the frame of my bike, screwed the cable to the valve and began pumping vigorously. It took only moments to establish where the puncture was, as a loud flappy hiss identified the tear in the innertube wall.

'It's going to take at least two of these patches to mend that, it's a big tear!' he declared, and began searching through his small bag of tools as the rest of us peered at the gaping hole in the flaccid pink innertube.

Ten minutes or so later he had finished. With some help too from Robert and Hicks, the puncture had been repaired, my tyre reinflated, and with no sign of further air loss we were on our way once more.

Some of the boys had taken advantage of the short break to snack on biscuits and sandwiches. I was unable to get to my saddlebag as my bike was turned upside down whilst it was being repaired. This was possibly a good thing, as I might well have finished off my two remaining egg sandwiches – which would have only left me with a Wagon Wheel and two buttered cream crackers.

The Needles

Although the day had started overcast it was becoming brighter and warmer. As the last of summer traced its fingers through my hair, we cycled in convoy along the Yarmouth Road that took us directly and easily down into Yarmouth itself. We were soon crossing the bridge over the River Yar, all of us looking forward to the fast descent of Halletts Shute, when disaster struck once more.

The front wheel of my bike began to wobble uncontrollably and my immediate instinct was to jam on the brakes. This had the effect of throwing me both forward and sideways onto the banked grassy verge, luckily narrowly missing a swathe of gorse bushes. The crashing metallic sound of sliding bicycle together with the sight of flying egg sandwiches, buttered cream crackers and bits of Wagon Wheel filled the air as at last, but certainly not least, I landed heavily amid this carnage. After what seemed an eternity, boys' faces began appearing, looking down at me, at first enquiring as to my state of health and wellbeing and then one by one informing me that my bike had suffered yet another puncture.

Mike and Hicks were busy trying to straighten my handlebars while Sherf and Robert were attending once more to the punctured front tyre. Two magpies had flown down from one of the hawthorn trees that bordered the adjoining fields and were behind a gorse bush fighting over one of the egg sandwiches.

'I think this innertube is buggered. I'll try my best to patch it up, it's another big tear,' said Sherf as he stood, hands on hips, looking down despairingly at the limp pink tongue of the innertube hanging from the side of the front wheel tyre.

'I think the whole tube is perished,' noted Robert. 'It's just like paper, it's falling to bits. If we get this thing patched up enough to hold air it will be a bloody miracle.'

Whilst the debate on the permanence or otherwise of the innertube was taking place, I stood gazing at the remnants of my sandwiches, still being fought over by the magpies. My elbows and knees were reminding me of just how hard I must have hit the road when I had fallen from my bike.

'You're bleeding old mate,' said Sherf, pointing to my knee.

After searching in the bottom of his saddlebags he passed me a tin of plasters.

'See Gussy, we did need the buggers after all, you just never know. The tyre seems to be staying up well enough though.'

'We'll leave it for a few more minutes for the glue to harden properly,' said Robert, squeezing the offending tyre between his finger and thumb.

'Yeah, it shouldn't be too long,' said Sherf. 'Then we will need to be ready to go, we're behind time again.'

After ten minutes, all of us having taken turns to place our ears close to the tyre before declaring unanimously that we were unable to discern a hiss or feel it softening in any way, it was decided that it was safe enough to continue our journey.

The more I thought about my lost sandwiches and buttered crackers the hungrier I became. So much so that it was a relief to have the alternative pain of my bruised and battered legs and elbows. My plastered wounds were stinging and burning like fire as we pedalled quickly through the tiny village of Colwell, picking up Church Hill on our way down to Totland Bay. When we reached the crossroads that took us down to Alum Bay we stopped for a quick breather. We agreed that we would take the opportunity for a welcomed food and drink stop and a quick exploration of Alum Bay itself, together with its world-famous multi-coloured sand cliffs.

As the sea blew cooling light zephyrs of sea air into our faces, we stood amused to listen to an argument between Hicks and Mike. It emanated from a fact-enthused Mike that when his

Grandfather was a boy he had swum completely around the Needles, stopping at the furthest point of the lighthouse to share a beer with the lighthouse keeper himself before setting off to swim ashore.

'Bugger off!' shouted Hicks. 'I've met your old Grandad, he's not big enough to pick up a bottle of beer never mind being able to swim round the Needles. You don't half come out with bullshit!'

'Not him,' agreed Mike. 'I'm talking about my other Grandad, my Mum's Dad. They say when he was a youngster, he was a champion swimmer. They say he once swam from Ryde Pier over to Gilkicker Point.'

'Where?' barked Hicks, in obvious disbelief.

'Gilkicker Point,' repeated Mike. 'It's not far from Pompey!'

'Oh bugger off! Like I said, it's all bullshit, nobody could swim over Spithead from Ryde Pier against those currents.'

At that, Hicks closed his mouth – much to our relief – over a pork pie and began opening a bag of crisps.

Happy in the sound of my companions' loud mass mastication, apples and crisps crunching, the ever-present smell of egg sandwiches (alas, not mine), the gurgle-down gulps of lemonade, lips smacking as orange juice and ginger beer were being savoured and swallowed, I sat with maddening self-loathing and regret at my own greed before the day's adventure had hardly begun. My dark, self-piteous gloom was broken through by Mike offering me a swig of his Mother's homemade lemonade along with a cheese and tomato roll, then an offer of a corned beef sandwich and pickled onion from Hicks, and finally a piece of fruit cake from Robert.

As I thanked them for their generosity, I pondered on the likelihood of my own ability to share as easily had the shoe been on the other foot.

We had laid our bikes upon the grassy cliff top, close to the winding path that the led down through the layers of coloured sands before it reached the stony beach. We sat for nearly an hour gazing across to the Needles. An amazing view of three jagged chalk white rocks climbing almost 100 feet out from the Solent and at its most westerly point. (As a matter of interest, the most westerly point of the Isle of Wight is a lighthouse painted like a barber's pole.)

'They do say,' announced Hicks, our gang's most well-read and cleverest boy, 'that there used to be four rocks out there once upon a time. The one that's missing was a big, tall, thin bugger and because it looked a bit like a needle, before it collapsed in the sea in some big storm a couple of hundred years ago, *all* the rocks here were known as the Needles and now the name has stuck. The real name of the missing rock,' he continued, 'was Lot's Wife,' and at this point Hicks looked to the heavens and shrugged, 'I think she was somebody famous in The Bible. Anyway, it was just there,' he continued, quite excited and animated, determined to show us all exactly where the missing rock once stood and pointing his finger towards the obvious gap, 'can you see... it's there, there, just there.'

Sherf and Robert were otherwise occupied, talking in loud whispers. They were stood beside the heap of cycles laid on the grass, both shaking their heads in incredulous dismay.

'What's up?' shouted Mike.

'Sorry to say, but Gussy's bike has got yet another puncture,' shouted back Sherf, 'and this time it can't be mended.'

'Why?' we all chorused as one.

Still shaking his head, Robert was the first to speak.

'It's the tyre's air valve. You know, where you pump it up. Well, it has come away from the innertube and because the whole innertube is bloody perished it just can't be fixed.'

The realisation of Robert's words echoed in my head. For one moment, I was sure that I must be dreaming and imagining everything, and in the blink of an eye I would suddenly wake up. Here I was in Alum Bay, at least twenty miles from home, staring out across to the wonderous and majestic view of the world-famous Needles. Places I had only heard of. Unbelievably, although I had been born and bred an islander, I had never seen them. Overners that visited the island for a week or so during the summer saw much more of the Isle of Wight than I ever had. The back of the island might as well have been the Mediterranean.

Sherf, Robert and I were in frantic debate concerning the calamitous series of punctures that had befallen the oh-so-unlucky accursed Girl's Bike and the likelihood that the sodding thing was going to have to be pushed back home to East Cowes. Whilst we had been talking about the dilemma, we had failed to notice that both Hicks and Mike were cycling off towards the beach. They had decided to cycle down the precarious winding sandy cliff path on their bikes in search of some glass containers from the souvenir shop in which they could gather up small quantities of the many shades of coloured sands. Hicks, who had presented himself as the aficionado of all things 'West Wight', had informed Mike that there were at least twenty-one different shades of sand within the cliff face to be found.

'Some of the colours of sand are rarer than others,' Hicks told him. 'I happen to know and on good authority,' he continued, as he tapped his nose in an above-board fashion, 'that people will pay good money to get all twenty-one colours in one of those lighthouse or Isle of Wight shaped glass containers.'

That was incentive enough for Mike as he crabbed sideways one way and then another, ever closer towards the beach.

When the two boys returned, red faced and breathless after their steep climb back from the beach, they were empty handed as there had been no glass containers to purchase. Instead, they had spent what little money they had between them on ice cream, sweets and twenty Player Weights cigarettes.

'You two have been bloody ages where did you get to?' said Sherf in one breath.

'Just down on the beach,' wheezed Mike, still gasping from the exertion of the hill climb. 'We went down to climb up into the cliff for some of the coloured sand. I bet you didn't know that some of the rarer colours fetch good money if you can find them.'

'Bullshit!' shouted Robert, who began laughing loudly and pointing an accusing finger at Hicks. 'You sure you haven't been telling those fairy tales again?'

For the next few hours, smoking Hicks's cigarettes, we spent our time not so much on the problem of a dead bike but more on the merits of air pistols and air rifles and the ability and skills required to make powerful catapults even more powerful. As the day drew on, black corn flies began swarming and flying into the humid mid-afternoon's warm air from the interior of the island. The darkening sky took on a ghostly luminosity as the first flash and crash of thunder shook the very ground on which we sat and the first heavy splat of a raindrop as it bounced off the sun-baked ground.

The deluge of rain and hail lasted for no more than ten minutes, but it was enough time to flood, thoroughly soaking everything and everybody that was close by. Stormwater was gushing and roaring in torrents down every ravine in the cliff face. The close by sea and Needles were no longer able to be seen from our position on the cliff tops. We all watched in awe as the storm drifted westward, smoking out over where we supposed the Needles were in thin grey curtains, slowly dipping down into the sea.

Peril and Plans

Sat as we were on the grassy verges of the open cliff top's viewing area, we had no shelter from the torrential rain and hail and little time to scramble through our saddlebags to retrieve our trusty rolled-up plastic pac-a-macs, which at the peak of the cloudburst would have afforded us little protection. We were all without exception soaked to the skin and to make matters worse there was a distinct cooling chill carried by the lingering squall. The late summer storm had left us little choice but to think of nothing other than making realistic plans of how returning home, pushing a wounded girl's bike, could be made possible.

Following a noisy discussion related to all things homeward bound, it was unanimously agreed that Sherf and Robert were likely to be the quickest. They would make the journey home as soon as possible to ensure that a rescue of sorts could be planned, probably via Sherf's Dad who could hopefully arrange transportation to pick up us suffering and weary stragglers.

Mike and Hicks had bravely volunteered to accompany me, taking turns to walk and ride together, whilst I was left pushing my trusty iron steed homeward. My task was made the more tedious due to the constant rattle and wobble of the front wheel caused by my forlorn and broken borrowed bike's flat tyre. In order to keep our spirits up we sang loudly and at one point tried to thumb a lift from a passing open truck, but to no avail.

It had been two hours or so since Robert and Sherf had set off to East Cowes. We estimated they should have reached home by now and were hopefully organising some help. We were exhausted and although we had dried off considerably through walking, we were still quite damp from our drenching. We calculated that the total mileage from Alum Bay to East Cowes was at least twenty miles and were devastated when we discovered that we were only a couple of miles past Yarmouth, which left another fourteen miles or so ahead of us.

Before setting off we had agreed that we, the walkers and pushers, would return homewards by keeping to the main road routes heading toward Newport. The task of discovering us, should a rescue happen, would therefore be made easier. After another hour or so had passed we were struggling from exhaustion and hunger, but at least we were well past Shalfleet. The evening's cloudy sky had begun turning rose pink and gold, slipping across the horizon in streaks behind the thin blue edge of the mainland.

All vestiges of food and drink had long gone and sadly we had all enjoyed the last of Hicks's cigarettes more than a couple of miles further back. Now that we were quickly losing the daylight, we took the sensible precaution to walk in single file. We endeavoured to keep each other interested and focussed on the task in hand by talking and arguing the pros and cons of a wide breadth of subjects. One of the more memorable being "Why do girls' bikes have no cross bars?", which was quite a lengthy discussion, but with no sensible or polite conclusion. Then followed the pros and cons of the latest pop music scene, which grew into a loud and lively debate as Hicks demonstrated his Elvis Presley impersonations. Mike, not be left out, shook his blond locks liken to that of Tommy Steele as he sang he had "never felt more like singin' the blues".

Sherf and Robert had maintained an excellent pace, despite the large areas of flood water on the roads which had affected the whole island. At times when the road was clear they had raced each other, competing to be the first to reach the chain ferry as they had elected to cycle home via the direct route to West Cowes. On their way to the ferry, they too had seen the sun dipping down behind the stormy clouds over Calshot Spit as they had passed in the shadow of the silver leviathan of the cocooned Princess Flying Boat, grounded forever as she stood tied down upon the Solent Works slipway on Medina Road. The crossing on the chain ferry to East Cowes was chilly, the wind whipping off the Medina raw as it blew cold against their still damp clothes. Both boys stood astride their bicycles as they leaned forward over their handlebars, edging slowly ever forward to the closed prow gate to ensure they would be first off when the gates opened and the ramp started to descend, ready for the race from uphill to Sherf's house 'Shalimar' on York Avenue.

As they sprinted, heads down, bodies arched, legs flying, racing madly one against the other as though it was the Tour De France itself, they pushed on even harder uphill. They suddenly became aware of loud whoops and shouts as they drew closer to Sherf's house. Slowing for a moment, they could not believe what they saw. Through the fading light they could make out a small crowd consisting of my Mother, together with all the other parents and siblings, all shouting at the same time, their arms outstretched in joy as they huddled together outside of Mr and Mrs Sherfield's bungalow.

Following breathless explanations to the concerned parents, a plan was quickly formulated to pick up and rescue us stragglers. Once we had been found, the bikes would be dismantled and Mike and Hicks would come home with Mr Brinton in his old Morris van whilst the girl's bike and me would travel back with Mr Sherfield in his small Hillman Minx.

It was in the chilling edge of late summer darkness when they found us. I can remember seeing a confusion of flashing headlights, torches and beams, immediately followed by loud instructions from Mr Sherfield and Mr Hicks as they set to with spanners to ensure we were able to remove our bikes' front wheels. The rescue could not have been timelier as the coldness was beginning to seep into the marrow of our bones. I recall the joyous comfort and smell of horse blanket as it was draped over my shoulders. Through our chattering teeth, the heavenly pleasure of flasks of hot sweet tea and beef paste sandwiches that had been kindly made by Mrs Hicks and Mrs Sherfield helped to fight off the urge to shiver and shake.

It would be several days later before the cramping aches in everyone's legs had begun to diminish. Not forgetting my own grazed knees and elbows, which were healing, but still bruised and sore.

High in a tree camp, built in a sycamore tree, past the Bommy Building, through the thickets in the field that edged Warner's Farm, the gang of five, lit by candles, met again.

The excited shrill of boys all needing to be first to tell and retell the tale that dwelt upon the rescue by Mr Sherfield together with the other fathers, quickly followed by endless versions of the adventure we had undertaken. The fact that we had only got as far as Alum Bay and the Needles did not make it any less adventurous or exciting.

We all told differing stories of how we had survived the biggest storm ever to hit the Isle of Wight since the old King died and how three of us were left to face the walk of a lifetime. My particular walk, of course, being a walk of shame, as I had been the reason we were all in that situation. We all enjoyed hearing the details again and again of how the rescue had been put into action, as Sherf and Robert took it in turns to retell and embellish the story of the gang of five's 'Round the Island Cycle Trip'.

Little did I know that was to be my last summer on the Isle of Wight for quite some time, or that it would be the last time I would be sat enjoying the smoke and candlelight of a tree camp. Neither had I any idea whatsoever that it was the last time I would ever see my friends again as boys. Although I had thought no more about the nightmare of the recent bicycle trip, it would be the last time I would ride a girl's bike.

Comes the Day, Comes the Sixpence

Comes the day, comes the sixpence
Solent shells upon silver shingle
White racing August clouds are drifting

Comes the day, comes the sixpence
White horses dancing to furthest indigo
Comes the day, now here's a shilling

Comes the day, comes the sixpence
Salt-kissed rocks in quiet pools of green
Now the squalling rain in curtains

A penny for your thoughts nipper

Epilogue

It was only a few months later, after autumn had shimmered gold and red into drear November and Christmas was drawing ever closer and the chill of winter had begun, that my Father sadly learned the meaning of the word 'Redundancy'.

Undeniably one of the biggest employers on the island, Saunders and Rowe was suffering from decisions taken by the board concerning curbing the building and development of flying boats and other light aircraft, together with what was soon to become the company's white elephant – that of the Princess Flying Boat Airliner. Recently they had been investing and developing in the Skeeters, soon to become the SARO Helicopters project, whilst at East Cowes the main board chose instead to develop and demonstrate the first working hovercraft.

Saunders and Rowe was deeply sorry to have to shed their skilled workers in such a shocking manner. However, they did endeavour to find as many of the those who had been made redundant alternative employment. My Father had been offered new employment with the national company ICI, which was a mammoth chemical complex situated on the outskirts of Middlesbrough in the north east of England. And as different from the Isle of Wight as chalk is to cheese.

A few weeks after Easter I watched the Isle of Wight fade slowly into the sea and sky as I hung over the rail upon the deck of the old paddle steamer *Ryde*. It was taking my Mother, Father and myself from Ryde Pier Head to Portsmouth and from there we were to go on by train to Waterloo.

The London Underground was indeed an eyeopener to three Caulkheads like ourselves. Nonetheless, after pushing our way through crowds of fellow passengers' suitcases and escalators, we were finally at King's Cross railway station ready for the